Candle Power

Candle Power

Using Candlelight for Ritual, Magic and Self-discovery

Cassandra Eason

BLANDFORD

Candles are living flames and as such require the same precautions as any other source of fire. Ensure that your candles cannot be knocked over and that there is no chance of fire should you drift off to sleep: a candle in an enclosed glass holder, a night light in a lantern or a candle floating on a bowl of water are all safe options.

A BLANDFORD BOOK

First published in the United Kingdom 1999 by Blandford

Text copyright © 1999 Cassandra Eason

The moral right of Cassandra Eason to be identified as the author of this work has been asserted in accordance with the UK Copyright, Designs and Patents Act 1988.

Distributed in the United States of America by
Sterling Publishing Co., Inc.
387 Park Avenue South
New York, NY 10016-8810

A CIP catalogue record for this book is available from the British Library

ISBN 0-7137-2767-5

Candles for illustrations supplied by Price's Candles, 10 York Road, London SW11 3RU.

Designed and typeset by Ben Cracknell Studios

Photography by Mike Newton

Printed by Dah Hua Printing Press Co. Ltd, Hong Kong

Blandford
Illustrated Division
The Orion Publishing Group
Wellington House
125 Strand
London WC2R 0BB

Contents

Introduction: Entering the World of Candles   6

A TRADITION OF **CANDLES**

1   History, Myth and Superstition   7
2   Candle Festivals   13
3   Rites of Passage   22

BEGINNING **CANDLE MAGIC**

4   Candle Colours   30
5   Candle Fragrances   40
6   Endowing Candles with Power   45
7   Protective Candles   59
8   Candle Rituals   65
9   Seasonal Candle Magic   71
10 Candle Magic for All Occasions   85

CANDLES AND PSYCHIC DEVELOPMENT

11 Candles and Meditation   92
12 Candles and Astral Projection   97
13 Candles and Divination   104
14 Candle Magic and Past Lives   113

FORMAL **CANDLE MAGIC**

15 Candles and the Elements   123
16 Creating a Special Place for Candle Magic   130
17 Formal Candle Ceremonies   136

Further Reading   143
Index   144

Candles are magical. They add warmth and atmosphere to a special meal, and gently soothe restless children to sleep. They can invoke moments of quiet reflection, or help us to access the deep wisdom that lies beyond conscious thought. They can be used in ritual as a focus for our most powerful dreams, hopes and desires.

Every child who wishes on a birthday candle shares in the rich mythological tapestry of the earliest peoples, who kindled tallow torches to illuminate the darkness of the cave or mark a way across a lonely pass; such wish candles connect us across the ages to the peasants and landowners alike who carried blazing torches around fields in procession at one of the ancient agricultural festivals, invoking the power of the sun to bring fertility to humans, animals and the land. These festivities in turn link with the lonely candlelit vigils of women who once sat hour after hour by the bedside of a sick child or dying relation, in that mesmeric half-sleep, half-waking state wherein true insight lies.

The life of man is said to be like a candle – the candle itself the mortal form, the unburned wax undeveloped potential and its flame the spirit – for candles are not only light, but living fire. When a candle is spent or we snuff it out, the light may be gone from our external vision and the warmth from our touch, but that light is not lost: rather, it is transformed into radiant beams that fuel the positive energies of the universe and fall as love and healing on those who gaze into a candle flame in sorrow, pain or fear.

Before you read this book, turn off the lights and spend a few silent minutes by candlelight, connecting with the older, slower and wiser rhythms that are not divided into months, years or even millennia, but flow in cycles and release us from the treadmill of time. Unlike the starkness of electricity, which makes night as bright as day and prevents our bodies from tuning into their natural ebbs and flows, candle power slows both the conscious mind and the body as night falls or in the hours around dawn, as new energies and enthusiasm return with waking. It is in this hiatus that the more intuitive parts of our mind come to the fore, releasing the inspiration within us.

As you light your candle now, you automatically interact with people around the world who light candles or torches as dusk falls. If you have a loved one or friend far away you can 'send' the light to them, even across oceans. Where there is estrangement, send forgiveness and your own regrets in the light. And if you choose a regular time – perhaps once a week – for you and the absent person to light your candles, you can meet telepathically within the flame.

Each candle is part of an interconnected cosmic web of millions of tiny beams, and as you look through the candle flame you may see on the other side someone smiling back at you through their light – a familiar face, someone you have yet to meet, or a stranger – across time and space, an hour, a day or perhaps thousands of years away.

PART ONE

A Tradition of *Candles*

CHAPTER ONE

History, Myth and Superstition

The flickering flame of the candle provides us with a link to the sacred flames that have been kindled over thousands of years. Palaeolithic man, who created hollowed stone lamps and tapers from animal fat with juniper twigs, used candles and lights as a way of illuminating not only living quarters, but also the inner sanctuaries that extended from cave dwellings and were decorated with tapers in honour of the Mother Goddess.

Beeswax candles were also used in Egypt and Crete as early as 3000BC and were a feature of worship in many pre-Christian societies. Bees were regarded as messengers of the gods and goddesses, and so candles made from their wax were seen as forming a precious link between mortals and the heavens. In the Christian tradition, beeswax candles have become associated with the Virgin Mary.

Today, many people use only beeswax candles for magical and spiritual development, and these are available not only in yellow but also dyed with natural vegetable colourings. However, you can perform candle magic with white utility candles and it will be as pure and true as if you had followed the lists of colour correspondences, fragrances and herbs that are included in this book. These can add ceremony, atmosphere and create a mood of harmony in which conscious barriers dissolve, but those who say that the tools are magic in themselves, rather than just adornments and a means of accessing our innermost powers, are mistaking fantasy for true spiritual experience.

Living *by candlelight*

Although we would not wish to recreate the harsh world of our ancestors, nevertheless at weekends or when you have two or three spare days, especially during the winter, it can be a restorative experience to rise with the sun, then as dusk falls, to light candles, and, when they have burned to nothingness, go to bed.

Before the advent of gas and electrical lighting, autumn and winter were the time of shorter days and longer evenings and nights. The body fell naturally into a slower rhythm until the spring, when lighter days called it back to a full peak of activity. Today, with phones, faxes and pagers constantly jostling for our attention, it is extremely difficult to step back into those quieter ways. But if, even for a short period, you can manage to avoid all electrical appliances and spend quiet, calm, candlelit evenings in the company of family and friends, you will find tensions slipping away and relationships improving.

Candle **time**

The old candle clocks – at their simplest, a tall candle divided into equal units – offered a way of telling how much time had elapsed. Although we now have far more accurate ways of recording time, candle time is still of great value. For example, when family members or the people you share a flat with are split by some seemingly insoluble grievance, you can set aside 'candle time' to discuss it.

○ Take a small candle and gently etch regular intervals in it, dividing it into parts for each person involved.
○ Choose a quiet time and gather everyone together. By the warm, soft light of this candle, each person should be allowed to speak uninterrupted while the candle burns through their section.
○ After all the candle units are gone, the candle should be blown out and the light 'sent' to strengthen those who have talked by candlelight.

Talking by the light of a single candle can help to remove the confrontational nature of harsh lighting and allows each person to talk, shielded by darkness. Tones are softer, emotions and vulnerability more easily expressed. Often, by simply waiting to voice annoyance or criticism until the candle is lit and the parties seated, the anger of a moment can pass or become muted, and the true issues be resolved.

Candle time need not be used only in cases of confrontation. Modern families rarely sit down together – even partners will often eat at different times before rushing on to another activity. If you can make a candle time even once a week, then two people can sit and talk or even contemplate together in silence – *being* not doing – and recall the reasons that their relationship was created and still endures.

Even the most seemingly insoluble dilemma or resentment can be limited to a weekly candle period, and when the unit is burned down the matter is put aside for another week, so that it does not eat away at all the energies needed for your daily life.

Candles **and magic**

The first magical rituals recorded are those of the Egyptians, who in the third century BC used candles to induce creative dreams. In this tradition, called 'dreaming true', someone with a question of great importance went to a cave that faced south and sat in the darkness, gazing at the candle flame until they saw in it a deity. They would then sleep, and in their dreams (it was said) the god or goddess would bring the answer to the problem.

Like the Egyptians, you can use a candle to get in touch with your deep, unconscious wisdom. Some believe that through such methods we can also access the great tribal wisdom, the collective knowledge of mankind in all times and in all places.

- Choose a quiet place after dark, if possible facing south – the direction of light and illumination – in the old tradition.
- Light a large white candle and sit with your eyes half-closed, gazing into the flame. If you want to blink or close your eyes do so, as it is important that you are calm and relaxed.
- Breathe regularly and deeply. Visualize the light of the candle entering your body with each breath, illuminating your inner being. Let the question run though your mind like a gentle mantra. Make no effort to consider options or to use conscious thought processes.
- You may see a figure, either in your mind's eye or in the candle flame: perhaps an archetypal wise person, a Chinese sage, a monk, a nun or an angel. This may be your spirit guide or guardian, whom you have seen in dreams or been attracted to in literature or history. Other people believe that what we see at such moments of stillness is our higher evolved self, which connects us with the realms of the spirit. Once you have identified your figure, blow out the candle, asking silently that the wisdom they have to impart may come to you while you sleep.
- Take a bath, adding no more than ten drops of lavender, geranium or rose essential oil for harmony to the water. Read the instructions given on the oils, as some are very potent and should only be used sparingly or not in pregnancy, although the three I have named are very gentle and safe. Lie quietly in bed in candlelight, until you feel ready to sleep. After you have blown out the candle, watch the after-images in the dark.
- When you wake, make a note of any symbols you saw in your dreams, for they will hold the key to your question, even if you do not recall your guardian. Write down what each symbol suggests to you, without trying to rationalize what it ought to mean – if in doubt, weave a story around them to provide an outcome.

In medieval Europe, the Christian use of candles did not entirely obliterate the earlier beliefs in their magical properties. For example, farmers would set candles that had been blessed by priests to guard livestock from danger and from the supposed malevolence of witches – often harmless, albeit eccentric, old ladies in the village, who would be blamed for a bad harvest or an epidemic.

Candle and pin magic for love
Traditionally, a lovestruck girl would call her lover to her by piercing the wick of a lighted candle with two intertwined pins, saying:

> *'Tis not these pins I wish to burn,*
> *But my lover's heart to turn,*
> *May he neither sleep nor rest,*
> *Till he has granted my request.*

The maiden would then watch the candle, and if the pins remained in the wick after the candle had burned past the place at which they were inserted, the lover would appear at the door before the candle burned down. If the pins fell out, it was taken as an indication that the man was faithless. In another version, two

pins were stuck in a candle for two alternative lovers and when the candle burned down to the correct pin, the door would open and the true lover would walk in – or at least a vision of him.

While we should not try to draw someone to us against their will, nor to bind a lover who does not wish to remain, candle and pin love spells do have a place in modern magic. Although historically they tended to be practised by young girls, these rituals are equally potent if followed by men. They can be used to send out attracting vibes to someone unknown who would make you happy; or, if you have a secret yearning for someone you know but have been too uncertain to reveal it, candle love spells will carry your feelings telepathically where, if unconsciously desired by the other party, they can be acknowledged and reciprocated.

You should carry out this ritual on the new or waxing (growing) moon, which is good for all magic where increase is required.

- Take a green candle and place it in a candle holder on a heatproof tray. Use a good-quality candle that will not crack or crumble; beeswax is good, and takes the pins easily.
- Light the candle and, as it begins to soften, insert a pin very gently but firmly into the candle wick, saying in an adaptation of the age-old rhyme:

> 'Tis not this pin I wish to burn
> But a willing heart to turn
> Though I do not speak your name
> I call you love through candle flame.

- Sit quietly in the candlelight, and if the pin remains in the wick after the candle has burned past it, love should arrive within a relatively short time.
- Blow out the candle, sending the love to whomever will make you happy or to let a chosen person know of your feelings. You may dream of your lover.
- If the pin falls out, it does not mean that love will not come, merely that you may need a little more patience, or perhaps that other areas of your life are temporarily taking priority. Repeat the spell on subsequent nights, inserting the pin even more tightly into the wick until it does stick.
- If you meet someone new to whom you are instantly attracted or see the person you secretly admire, make a friendly overture and – if it is right for you – some positive response may follow. If not, wait. Having sent your potential love into the cosmos, you must give it time to develop. Candle time is slow but often sure.

Candle curses

As with all magic, candles are neutral and have been used for evil as well as good purposes. But, again as with all magic, candle magic for negative purposes rebounds threefold on the sender, and so candle rituals should only be carried out if you are in a positive state of mind or with pure intent.

Bad witches would name a black candle after an enemy, let the wax fall and form a doll from it, then stick pins in this while letting the candle burn away.

Beeswax candles release a timeless honeyed fragrance.

Sticking pins in candles: *a modern interpretation*

Whether used for banishing bad habits, getting rid of guilt or to end a period of sorrow or bad luck, candle and pin magic can be a potent affirmation of intent. Because of past negative connotations, you should not use black candles – although in modern magic they refer only to natural endings – nor make a wax image of a person. Instead, abstract the quality or situation you wish to end by creating a waxen square, the magical shape of limitation.

This ritual works best in the late evening on the waning (diminishing) moon, which is good for all forms of decreasing or banishing magic.

○ Either in words or in your mind, endow a long pin with the feeling of whatever it is you wish to lose, holding it between your hands and saying:

Sharp pangs cease
Hard times end,
Into the candle flame,
Bend, pin, bend.

○ Light a purple candle for wisdom and spirituality, and as the wax softens, pierce the wick with the pin about 2.5cm (1in) down the candle, saying:

Burn, candle, burn,
Turn, sorrow, turn,
From pain to joy,
Bad times destroy,
Burn, sadness, burn.

○ Leave the pin hanging quite loosely and place a fireproof tray beneath the candle holder to catch the hot pin when it falls.

○ Burn tiny pieces of dark wool in the candle flame, naming a sorrow, a disappointment or a regret in each, and as each is burned say:

It is gone
It is done,
No more to return,
Burn, candle, burn.

○ Wait until the pin falls from the candle and catch a small piece of molten wax on the tray. Say:

Pin fall,
Do not recall
The pain you caused,
Pin die,
Let my
Heart be
Free
From your thrall,
Burn candle all.

○ As the fallen wax cools, roll it into a square to mark the limitations of the sorrow, and if you wish mark it with a cross as a final banishing gesture.
○ Let the candle burn down, and as it does so write on pure white paper positive steps for the future.
○ In the morning, bury the square of wax in a pot of earth and plant fast-growing seeds or seedlings of fragrant plants, so that daily you can see new life and hope growing.
○ Dispose of the blackened pin in a environmentally friendly way – make sure it goes somewhere it cannot pierce anyone – and take the first practical steps towards your new beginning.

How much of the ensuing illness or misfortune was due to the malice of feeling transmitted and how much to the person knowing of the curse and fulfilling it unconsciously, is hard to estimate. In Chapter 7 I do suggest protective rituals with candles: not against these ancient black magic curses, however, but to counter the everyday negative feelings that others can consciously or unconsciously transmit or bring home. Remember, though, that few who act maliciously ultimately achieve happiness or peace.

The most infamous kind of candle was the 'hand of glory' – the hand of a hanged man, squeezed dry, pickled for two weeks in saltpetre and left to dry in the sun; candles made from the fat of a hanged man were then attached to the fingers. This hand was traditionally used by thieves, for it was believed that if they lit one in a house, the occupants would sleep while the burglary was taking place.

CHAPTER TWO

Candle Festivals

Few festivals seem complete without candles – from the tiny coloured candles on a birthday cake to the giant versions carried by the penitents in the processions of Semana Santa, the Holy Week in Spain. It is little wonder that candles are so deeply ingrained in us, as they date back across millennia to those early celebrations at the midwinter solstice – the shortest day – when our prehistoric ancestors lit bonfires and illuminated their caves with tallow candles to persuade the sun to return. The festivals described in the following pages are not just quaint folk customs but lie at very the heart of our collective tribal memory.

If we can invoke some part of the deep spirituality that lies behind these candle rites, perhaps by recreating one of the old candle festival symbols or lighting a candle to recall the festivals that neighbours of different faiths and cultures may celebrate, then we can enter into an awareness that we are all interconnected at the very deepest level. Just as many non-Jewish families light candles as the weekend begins to greet family members home on Friday evenings, so non-Christians can derive great significance from the old midwinter candle traditions as light returns to the world.

Christmas/*Yule*

Light was the focus of the early midwinter solstice around 21 December, from which the modern festival of Christmas derives. Whether one celebrates the birth of the unconquerable sun or the nativity of the Son of God, candles symbolize new life and hope at the darkest, coldest times. Hence many of the festivals of light cluster around mid-December and the end of January/beginning of February, the coming of spring in the old Celtic calendar.

Christmas candles

It is probable that some Christmas candle rituals have their roots in the Jewish winter festival of light, CHanukkah, described on page 19. Others stem from the nature religions that Christianity was grafted on to in the northern hemisphere.

Candles mark every stage of the Christmas celebration, beginning with the Advent candle and ending with the Twelfth Night candle to mark the last day of the festivities. By creating your own ongoing Christmas candle festival you can avoid focusing all your hopes on one single day, making it hard for it to live up to expectations. In times when money may be short and Christmas celebrations divided by the need to spend time with different sets of relatives – and in the case of divorce, different sets of parents – the candles can offer a continuous reminder of the spiritual focus of Yuletide.

Pause for a moment in the days before Christmas and sit either alone or with your family and friends by candlelight. No one really cares whether you make

Christmas candles recall the old winter festivals to celebrate the rebirth of light after the shortest day of the year.

your own mince pies or scour the shops for exactly the right gift that, however well received, may not always be appreciated. But these candlelit moments are precious, restoring your energies and, as with our ancestors, allowing you to withdraw in the cold of winter to your 'cave' to be with kin or to grow strong alone. It is what children will recall in years to come, long after they have forgotten the present that cost a small fortune. As you light your Advent candle, or any of the others over the coming days, make wishes for the future, share confidences about your feelings and fears, and tell the old stories in the twilight. Children especially love to make candle decorations and are not nearly so demanding if they can share in creating their Christmas rather than being passive recipients, excluded from the bustle and preparation that is an important part of any festivity.

THE ADVENT CANDLE

This was the forerunner of the present commercialized cardboard calendar with a chocolate behind each window, and is a custom worth reviving. An Advent candle, huge and scarlet or green, has 24 marks scribed on it. Though the date of Advent varies, beginning on the Sunday nearest to 30 November, traditionally a section of the candle is lit at dusk, starting on 30 November, and burned down by one mark each day, usually taking one or two hours.

You can make your own Advent candle by buying two large candles of the same size and seeing how far one of them burns in a hour. Then scratch 23 marks at similar intervals on the other, using a nail or rounded pen point. Light the last section at dusk on Christmas Eve and leave it to burn away; some people begin on 1 December, lighting their last section on Christmas Day itself.

The Advent candle can be used to light the other candles of the Christmas period. You can decorate the base with greenery, preferably gathered by you and your family or friends to endow it with the positive collective energies of the outing. An alternative is the Advent crown, a wire structure decorated with evergreen boughs and scarlet ribbons and holding four individual smaller Advent candles, one of which is lit on each of the four Sundays during Advent.

THE MIDWINTER SOLSTICE CANDLE

As well as bright scarlet Yule candles, you can burn beautiful golden and green candles, set in a circle of evergreens. Place a large golden candle in the centre of the circle to represent the new sun on the eve of the midwinter solstice.

Pick evergreen boughs, especially of pine or fir, just before dusk on solstice eve and surround your candle with lovely deep green stones such as aventurine, bloodstone or amazonite. If you have an open fire, you could scatter cedar, pine and rosemary on the logs, or burn these fragrances as incense.

Lighting the solstice eve candle continues a fire ritual practised for thousands of years and can form the focal point of a quiet evening with family and friends, enjoying a simple meal of winter root vegetables and one of the traditional meats of the season, and talking of your plans for the spring, telling the old family legends and perhaps reading pictures in the candle flame or on the shadowy walls as your ancestors did. If we can pass on a few of the old ways, then our descendants will be the richer.

THE CHRISTMAS EVE CANDLE

Traditionally, it is said to be very unlucky to leave a candle burning alone in a room, originally probably because of the fire risk. The exception is the Christmas Eve candle, which should be left burning all through the night of Christmas Eve in a safe place, in the hope that there will be sufficient light, warmth and food throughout the winter. This custom is a direct descendant of the old magical solstice ceremonies. Like the solstice candle, the Christmas Eve white candle should be surrounded by symbols of plenty: a small piece of coal or wood, a coin, and some grains and fruit or an ear of corn left from the harvest.

In Victorian times, and especially in the north of England until World War II, large candles were made specially for this purpose and presented by grocers, along with the Christmas order, to their best customers. In those times, the person deemed to be the head of the household or the oldest member of the family would light the Christmas Eve candle and extinguish it on Christmas morning.

During the medieval period and right up to the Industrial Revolution, any stranger who called at a house on Christmas Eve having seen the light would be made welcome in case he or she were Jesus or Mary. In Ireland, Brittany and among American families who have Celtic connections, the Christmas Eve custom of leaving a lighted candle in the window to light the Virgin Mary on her way survives. Food and drink is left in the kitchen for her.

It is sad that in modern times it is no longer safe to welcome strangers into our home, but you can continue the custom by inviting in a lonely neighbour or a student who is far from home. In France and French-speaking parts of Canada, families will light candles decorated with pine or fir branches during the *réveillon* or Christmas Eve dinner, eaten traditionally after Midnight Mass.

The Christmas Eve candle ensures that the festivities begin early and that no one is rushing around with last-minute chores. Children can receive a small candle gift, and lighting the candle can be a good ice-breaker.

CANDLES FOR THE TWELVE DAYS OF CHRISTMAS

In modern celebrations, the Yule log that in times past was kindled at the midwinter solstice with a charred piece of the previous year's log is usually replaced by scarlet candles, one for each day of the Twelve Days of Christmas from Christmas Eve to Twelfth Night. Or, in keeping with the older custom, a candle is burned each evening at dusk from the midwinter solstice eve onwards. The gold solstice eve candle was the first to be lit in this earlier practice.

Enjoy a final hour of fun as you put the decorations away for another year on Twelfth Night, and blow out your final Yule candle, sending love and light into the world and especially to absent or estranged members of the family.

CHRISTMAS TREE CANDLES

When were lights first hung on trees? Again, legend vies with fact. Originally, lights represented the sun, moon and stars on the 'cosmic tree', and later on the paradise tree that featured in medieval mystery plays.

My own favourite myth is that on 21 December, at the pagan midwinter solstice, St Boniface – who in the eighth century travelled from England to convert the Bavarians – encountered some Druids about to tie a young boy to a sacred oak and sacrifice him. Boniface chopped down the tree and behind it was a tiny evergreen. The Druids fell to their knees and hung their lanterns on the little tree. Of course, the legend has a strongly Christian bias, introduced by the monks who chronicled these stories. They were fuelled in their knowledge of apparent Druidic human sacrifice by Julius Caesar, himself hardly an unbiased recorder of the Celtic priesthood, which he saw as standing in the way of his conquests – not that the Romans who threw Christians to the lions had an unblemished record on human rights!

There is another, later, story that the first Christmas lights were placed on a fir tree by Martin Luther who, while walking towards his home one winter evening through a forest, was enraptured by the stars set against the brilliance of the evergreens. Anxious for his family to share his vision, he set up a tree at home with brightly twinkling candles among the branches.

There is no doubt that Christmas tree candles did cause many fires, and a bucket of water traditionally placed next to the tree served a dual purpose for watering the tree and in case of emergencies. Electric Christmas tree lights were created by Ralph E. Morris, an employee of New England Telephone, who in 1895 was inspired to his invention by the rows of lights on telephone switchboards!

Candlemas

Candlemas Day in the Christian calendar coincides with the anniversary of the purification of the Virgin Mary 40 days after the birth of Jesus, also the occasion when he was taken to the temple and hailed as the 'light of the world'.

On Candlemas Eve, blazing torches were carried clockwise around the still frozen fields and sacred fires lit on hilltops to attract the sun. On Candlemas Day, all the church candles that would be used for the coming liturgical year were blessed at High Mass. Blessed candles were also distributed to the congregation and the festival, like many others, was grafted on to the Celtic pre-Christian Feast of Lights, which was held on the three days from sunset on 31 January to sunset on 2 February. In the glorious mix of folklore and religion, the Candlemas candles were preserved at home because they were believed to have healing powers and, if rekindled, to act as a charm against thunder, lightning and earthquakes. On the following day, the feast of St Blaise, the newly sanctified church candles were used by priests to bless the throats of parishioners, so that they would be free from all respiratory illness in the coming months.

A family festival worth reviving in the often dark, cheerless days of winter is the lighting of a huge white candle on Candlemas night, or in earlier times Candlemas Eve, as the focal point for a family gathering and feast that continued until the candle burned out. The wax from this was sprinkled around the hearth and threshold to preserve the home from all harm for the coming year. Candles were then lit and placed in every window to hasten the warmer and lighter days.

Candlemas was also the day for predicting the weather and the arrival of spring. The US Groundhog Day on 2 February follows this tradition.

The Romans dedicated the feast day to the goddess Februs, when torches were carried down to rivers. The Celts called the festival Imbolc or Olmelc. Imbolc

Making your own candles: *a Candlemas ritual*

Although Candlemas is a holiday for professional chandlers, the evening of 31 January is the time for making domestic candles and those for magical purposes.

○ You can hold a candle-making party and then use the results to illuminate your home, either on the old Brigantia Eve (31 January) at dusk or on Candlemas Eve (1 February). Your Bride candles should be in beeswax, or any pastel shades, and you can make

a pretty garland around them of the first buds or greenery. Even young children can roll sheets of beeswax to make Bride candles.

○ Make one very large candle to serve as the main Candlemas candle, and as you light it allow everyone to make a secret wish for the coming spring.

○ As you make smaller candles to shine in every window, visualize each one being endowed with optimism for new beginnings, new directions and plans, and

name one for each absent family member or friend.

○ Prepare a feast that includes delicious seed breads and cakes, milk, honey, seeds of all kinds, lamb and dairy products, and spend the evening playing party games and charades.

○ If you have a decision to make, light two candles of the same size and thickness and endow each with an option. The one to burn down first indicates the right choice.

means 'in the belly of the Earth Mother', and so refers to the appearance of the first shoots of flowers and vegetation through the winter snows; Olmelc, translated as 'the feast of ewe's milk', refers to the first fresh milk available after the winter with the birth of the early lambs. In the days when any food can be acquired at almost any supermarket irrespective of the season, it can be important to try to link into the natural cycles of the year.

Yet another name for the festival was Brigantia, after the Celtic triple goddess Brigid or Bride, here in her maiden aspect replacing the Old Hag of winter's rule. She was Christianized as St Brigit of Kildare.

A spring equinox/Easter Eve *candle ritual*

This is a ritual to greet the return of the light and the rebirth of optimism, confidence and joy, and should be carried out after dusk.

○ Make or buy a very large pillar candle, yellow for the sun or pure white for light, endowing it with joy, health and energy for the coming months either during its making or by rubbing it with a special candle-anointing oil or pure olive oil, from the centre downwards and then from the centre upwards (see Chapter 5), listing out loud your hopes for yourself and those you love.

○ If the weather is fine, hold your ceremony in the open air, where you can light a small fire from as many different woods as you can find. If not, use an open hearth if possible, or tapers scented with honeysuckle or strawberry, associated with spring.

○ Kindle the source of fire and light your candle from it – a magical gesture that has been practised from the kindling of the early equinox fires onwards.

○ Surround the candle with any five spring flowers, such as crocuses, daffodils, hyacinths, primroses or violets, and five sticks or cones of spring equinox incense, such as

jasmine, rose, sage, thyme and violet.

○ As you light each incense stick with a taper from the candle, endow it with an affirmation of optimism, perhaps listing your own strengths, present joys or the names of supportive friends or family, saying:

As I light my first incense I recall how far I have already travelled towards creating/rebuilding my life in the way I wish.

As I light my second incense I recall my partner/friend [name] who has so loyally supported me and built up my belief in my power to succeed.

As I light my third incense, I recall my own ability to turn setbacks into challenges which I can take pride in overcoming and see obstacles as incentives to redouble my efforts.

As I light my fourth incense, I recall the pleasure I have derived from playing my guitar/gardening/walking in the countryside/playing with my children and recognize that these are just as worthwhile as achieving material recognition and success.

As I light my fifth incense, I reaffirm my determination to make the coming months fruitful and joyous for myself and those with whom I come into contact.

○ Between the flowers, place painted hardboiled eggs. Eggs were a symbol of spring and new life that were offered to Oestre, the Anglo-Saxon goddess, or Ostara, the northern goddess of spring, at the spring equinox; in Eastern Europe they were painted as offerings for the Virgin Mary. Name one egg for yourself and the rest for special friends or family members, endowing a gift of some strength or quality in each one.

○ Let the candle and fire, if you have one, burn down naturally. If possible, the next morning give the eggs to the people after whom they are named, to eat (according to magical tradition they will absorb the power of the wishes therein). If you are concerned about the health aspects of giving eggs to be eaten, keep them for a few days in a nest of flowers and greenery before burying them in the earth.

Easter candles: *the Paschal candle*

In the early Christian tradition, itself a relic of the old spring equinox, candles were extinguished on Easter Eve. The Paschal candle was then lit from the 'nyd' fire, which was kindled from nine different kinds of wood using an oaken spindle.

Bonfires were lit outside the churches and sometimes the effigy of a Judas man was burned. Charred sticks were taken from the fire and placed on newly kindled home fires or kept through the year as protection against thunderstorms. St Cyril of Jerusalem described the profusion of light on Easter Eve as being as bright as day, and Constantine the Great made the Easter Eve celebrations even more dazzling by placing lights not only in the basilicas, but also in the streets and squares. Homes were brilliantly illuminated with candles in every window to welcome the resurrection.

The Paschal candles of earlier times vied with one another in splendour and size. In 1517 the Salisbury Cathedral candle was 12m (36ft) in height, and in 1558, 152kg (3cwt) of wax was used for the Paschal candle in Westminster Abbey.

The Paschal candle was left standing upon the Gospel side of the altar from Holy Saturday until Ascension Day. Originally, the Easter Eve service was followed immediately by Mass shortly after midnight on Easter morning, but today the Paschal service is often held on Easter Eve morning.

CHanukkah

The Talmud, the body of Jewish oral law, decrees that beginning with the twenty-fifth of Kislev, which is approximately November–December on the conventional calendar, eight days of CHanukkah (or Hanukkah), the Festival of Lights, are observed. The extra-biblical holiday, Hanukkah, commemorates the Jews' victory over the Hellenist Syrians in 165BCE. After their victory, the Hasmoneans, or Maccabees, entered Jerusalem's Holy Temple, defiled by Syrian invaders, and cleansed it. They re-dedicated the temple to the service of God and celebrated the first Hanukkah – the Hebrew term for dedication – in memory of their victory.

The Maccabees wished to kindle the *menorah*, the seven-branched candelabrum which stood in the Holy Temple, but the Greeks had defiled all the oils. The Maccabees found only one small cruse (pot) of oil with the seal of the Kohen Gadol, the High Priest. Although it contained enough oil to burn for only one day, a miracle occurred and it burned for eight days. A year later the rabbis designated these days as Yomim Tovim, on which praise and thanksgiving were to be said.

In memory of the miracle of the Holy Temple menorah, a special menorah called a Chanukiah or Hanukkiya was created, and this is the origin of the special candelabrum used at the festival today. It is usually a nine-branched candelabrum whose candles are lit by a *shamash* or servant candle, which then takes its own place at the centre of the menorah. On the eve of CHanukkah, the shamash candle is lit first and used to light the first CHanukkah candle. One candle is

A personal candle festival **for abundance**

Candle festivals span many faiths and cultures. They not only celebrate or anticipate the return of light and warmth into the world, but by the feasting, sheer magnitude of light and offering of gifts, provide a religious-magic gesture that dates back to the dawn of time. By displaying abundance at a period of approaching dearth, the people who join in these celebrations are, consciously or unconsciously, asking that they will be given sustenance in hard times. Like the single cruse of oil in the Holy Temple, there will be sufficient, given a gesture of faith. Lakshmi, Hindu goddess of prosperity, is attracted to homes filled with light and colour: like attracting like is the basis of the most primitive forms of sympathetic magic, and yet lies behind the most spiritual of these celebrations of light.

You do not need to choose a recognized festival for your personal feast of lights, but can perform it on any occasion in your life when you need money, an increase in potential resources or greater opportunities.

○ Choose symbols of financial or professional increase taken from your present possessions: anything coloured gold or brass, gold-coloured coins, golden keys, any gold jewellery (whether genuine or gold-plated), even golden buttons or sequins. Place them on a large golden or brass dish or in a bowl covered with gold foil. Add talismans of natural abundance for increased fertility in the personal and emotional sphere: golden ears of corn, golden flowers or leaves, yellow seeds, even golden apples, so that the dish or bowl is completely full.

○ At dusk on the first day, light a golden candle where it can be seen from outside your home. If you cannot leave front windows uncurtained for security reasons, a back one will do just as well. Let the candle burn until it is completely dark. Look into the candle flame and see the golden symbols increasing and enveloping you in their abundance and fertility. When you are ready, blow out the candle, sending the light into the darkened world.

○ The next evening at dusk, light first a new golden candle and then the original one, again leaving them to burn until it is dark and blowing them out in the order you lit them. Let your thoughts be filled with golden light and optimism as you gaze into the flames.

○ Continue this for seven days, until the candles encircle the bowl, each dusk lighting first the new candle and then those from the previous nights. If any candles are burned down replace them, but keep to the day order in lighting, so that the last candle you light is always the one from the first day of the ritual. Each night as you stare into the flames, see your prospects improving. You may find that money-spinning ideas come to you in your dreams and by day your new confidence will open doors for you personally and professionally. Replace any flowers that have died or fruit that is becoming over-ripe. On the final day after you have blown out the last candle, leave them in position around the bowl until the following dusk.

○ On the eighth day, light what is left of the candles in different places around the house to spread the abundance. It is sometimes said that you should not use candles from rituals for everyday use, but I believe it is important that magic is not something set apart but should spread into and inspire the mundane, everyday world. Take what can be used from your golden bowl and bury or dispose of the rest.

○ If you cannot carry out this ritual at dusk, try to find a regular time each night for an unbroken period of seven days when you can light your candles. It is better to spend ten minutes each night rather than trying to rearrange your life and missing a session. The best magic will adapt to the real circumstances of daily living. Those who have the leisure to devote hours to developing their psychic awareness rarely need abundance in their lives – and need is the most powerful impetus of all.

added each night until all eight candles are present and lit. The Chanukiah is usually placed near a window or a door so that its warm light can be seen by passers-by on the street.

As the candles are lit and the blessings given, family and guests gather together and the candles continue to shine until they burn themselves out. Oil-based foods are part of the feasting in memory of the miracle of the Holy Temple oil.

This Festival of Light is, in a sense, continued each week, when the beginning of the Sabbath is marked in Jewish homes by the lighting of candles to greet the family and to draw them together. Eighteen minutes prior to sunset on Friday evenings, two white candles are lit, usually by the mother and daughters. After lighting them, they reach with their hands towards the candles and back to their eyes in a circular motion, three times. They then cover their eyes and a blessing is recited.

As mentioned already, the lighting of candles at the beginning of a weekend, even without the religious significance, is a very spiritual and loving custom. If you live far from family and friends, your candles are a way of connecting with them, especially if they light candles at the same time. Even if you have no one special in your life, your weekend candles can send love and positivity into the cosmos, directed to anyone with whom you may have a natural affinity. If you carry out this ritual regularly, you may find that within weeks you do meet a person or people with whom you can share friendship – or perhaps more.

CHAPTER THREE

Rites of Passage

The concept of our life as a candle was perhaps a very early metaphor as mankind saw candles burning for their allotted time, illuminating the darkness and, once spent, being replaced by another.

Candles were once an integral part of the rites of passage from birth to death, and there are many examples of this continuing tradition in everyday life and on special occasions. The most common is the birthday cake with its array of tiny candles; this custom stems from the festival of the Greek moon goddess Artemis, whose followers set candles on moon-shaped cakes to celebrate her feast day. As the candles were blown out, the celebrants consigned their wishes to the cosmos.

In contrast, the eternal flame burns in many different countries in memory of unknown warriors who died in foreign fields. In Catholic churches and some high Anglican cathedrals, candles can be bought and lit to ask for healing and comfort for the sick, and in memory of those who have died.

Candles have been used by the Church since the fourth century in rites of passage, beginning with baptism and ending with candles placed around the coffin at a funeral – a rite that dates back to the earliest belief that the dead needed protection from dark influences which lurked between the worlds.

The beginnings

At birth, too, candles would be lit around a newborn infant and his or her mother to protect them. In the Celtic tradition, after an infant was born, he or she was handed back and forth across a flame three times, from the midwife to the father. Prayers for blessing were then made to the power of the sun by the midwife, under her breath. The child was then carried deosil – sunwise or clockwise – around the flame three times by the father.

In the Isles of Orkney it was the custom to whirl a flaming torch of silver fir around the head of a mother and her newly delivered child to purify them: the silver fir is the tree of Druantia, the Gallic fir goddess.

As the traditional Christening service becomes less formal or is replaced by a naming ceremony, a candle is becoming a popular way to welcome a new infant. If there are other children in the family, the candle of the new baby can be added to a circle of candles for the other children. An informal candle welcoming ceremony, perhaps when the baby first comes home, is a good way of quashing any feelings of rejection by or in older children, as they see their candles lit first and the newcomer joining their light.

Birth candles

You can select a candle for an infant yet to be born, whether you are the parent to be, a grandparent or a family friend. Rather than buying an astrological candle –

Appropriate **candle colours**

White is the colour of the visionary and innovator, who will never lack energy or enthusiasm and will always adapt to the needs of the moment.

Red is the colour of the crusader, the campaigner who will never lack courage or determination to fight for what is important or for those he or she loves.

Orange is the colour of the joy-bringer, the integrator who can reconcile conflicting needs and priorities in self and others.

Yellow is for the communicator, the clear thinker, bringing order to chaos and certainty to doubt.

Green is for the loving heart, kind, sympathetic and with an understanding and acceptance of the frailty of others.

Blue is for the noble one, the creator and the bringer of justice, idealistic and altruistic.

Violet or indigo is for the mystic, the dreamer and the wise one, an old soul even from early childhood, whose gaze can pierce the veil that hangs between this world and the mysteries of the next.

Pink is for the peacemaker, the negotiator whose patience is endless, the healer of quarrels and harbinger of peace.

Brown is for the homemaker, the practical problem-solver, who brings security and warmth to the lives of others.

Silver is for the psychic, the clairvoyant, the healer of all ills and the prophet who guards secrets wisely.

Gold is the colour of the expansive one, the voyager who scans horizons physical, mental and spiritual, always seeking what is of true worth.

which, if the baby is early or late, may be of the wrong sun sign – close your eyes and let the vision of the essential infant come to you.

Alternatively, choose a candle colour from those listed above that embody different strengths. If two or three people choose candles for the same baby, the new infant may be endowed with several different gifts. Or, in true fairy godmother style, you can buy a selection of colours.

Choose a dozen or so of the same colour, shape and size that you can keep for birthdays and special landmarks in the child's life, such as going to school, beginning work or at graduation. You could make a special candlestick your Christening or naming gift.

When the mother goes into labour, light the baby's birth candle to ease the passage of the unborn infant into the world, and take or send one to the delivery suite to be lit after the birth. Endow the candle with all your hopes for the little one, and if you are not the mother, with love and protection for her. Once the baby is born, if you are not present, light a birth candle at home in welcome.

On each birthday, light the child's special candle, either as part of the celebration or alone, sending love and light to the child. When he or she is old enough, the little one should blow out the special candle and wish, remembering to keep the wish secret so that it will come true.

Candles for weddings or celebrations of **permanent commitments**

Over the years, weddings and celebrations of permanent commitments have, like baptisms, become less rigid and more personal. This has been helped along in the UK by the recent granting of the freedom to hold wedding ceremonies recognized by law in settings other than churches and register offices.

Welcoming a new family member

If your family is a close-knit one, then it can sometimes be difficult for an outsider to join. Someone marrying into the family, or the children of a new partner, can feel awkward or even excluded. In such cases, a simple ceremony of welcoming may help to ease the newcomer into the family circle.

○ Select a candle for each person, in either their astrological colour (see Chapter 4) or one that seems to embody their particular strengths. This can be a good way of identifying the positive qualities of each family member, including incomers.

○ Collect together symbols or photographs of all who are to be present. Place them on a large table, if the ceremony is to be held indoors, or in a suitable spot in the garden. Encircle the objects with tiny rose quartz or amethysts, or pink and lilac glass nuggets if you have no crystals; these are stones of harmony and reconciliation.

○ Dim the lights (if outside, perform the ceremony after dusk) and ask the oldest person present to light their candle. You are now going to enclose the symbolic family objects in a circle of candlelight. The oldest person should place their candle behind the photographs and/or symbols in the 12 o'clock or symbolic north position. Say words such as:

I welcome [name] who has illuminated our family for so long with wisdom and compassion.

○ Continue in age order, clockwise around the symbolic family, letting the incomer slot in naturally at the relevant age position. As each person lights a candle, welcome them and acknowledge the strengths they already contribute or will bring to the family circle. When all the candles are lit, let everyone stand behind their own candle, and say:

May we be encircled within mutual growing affection and let no intrusion by any who would see our family divided enter this ring of light.

○ Spend the evening together having a meal, talking, and leaving aside any divisive or controversial matters. Draw strength from the circle of light, and if anyone makes a thoughtless or sharp remark, repeat the affirmation of unity silently before answering.

○ When the candles have burned down, blow out one another's light, the eldest to the youngest, so that you absorb the love from each other's flame, and sit for a few moments in the darkness seeing pictures of happiness in the after-images. Say softly:

May the gentle darkness absorb any differences of opinion.

○ It may be helpful to repeat the ritual at monthly gatherings if possible, leaving all differences outside the circle of light. This regular non-confrontational gathering can form a firm foundation for developing unity, especially if you continue to emphasize positive qualities that may emerge and insist that no differences of opinion or grievances can be aired at the candle ritual.

Lighting candles and joining together two separate lights in a single flame forms a potent spiritual symbol of unity in both formal and informal commitment ceremonies. You can just as easily adapt the ritual for a private affirmation of intent with a lover. In the USA especially, the unity candle, as the large central candle is called, has become very popular. Two taper candles, representing the couple as individuals, are used to light a single central candle as a symbol of the union.

There are many variations of this candle ritual. Respective sets of parents can take their grown-up child's taper and light the central candle, as a sign that their son or daughter is moving to a new phase of life and a new adult commitment that will become even more binding than their role as child in the parental family. This gesture can be particularly potent if one or both sets of parents are finding

On the festival of Artemis, Greek moon worshippers placed candles on cakes – the first birthday wishes.

it hard to accept the child's new partner. However, many couples prefer to light the candle themselves from their individual tapers.

Some couples then extinguish the lighted taper, saying as they do so words such as these:

I am no longer separate but willingly unite in love, fidelity and trust. Henceforth we two are one.

This can be a good point for exchanging rings or love symbols.

Others leave the separate tapers burning as a sign that they will not be possessive towards each other or try to stifle the other's individuality within the relationship.

If the couple already have children either from the present or an earlier relationship, the children can have their own tapers as part of the ceremony, joining their flames momentarily to the central candle.

The children should leave their own tapers burning, perhaps encircling the main bridal candle, as an acknowledgement that they in their turn will one day fly the nest.

You may wish to rekindle a unity candle on your anniversaries, renewing your vows in a private ceremony with your loved one.

A *divorce or* **separation ceremony**

When a couple agree to part, a candle ritual can be a focus, either together or alone, for marking the beginning of the return to a new life as separate units but retaining affection for each other. This can be particularly important if there are children, and can help reconcile them to the parting.

○ A candle representing the couple should be ignited first, then separate tapers for the divorcing couple placed in the central candle flame and left burning on either side of it. The first candle can be extinguished with such words as:

The original flame of love that once united us has grown dim, and so we go our separate ways with regret, not bitterness, and with gladness for all the happy times we shared.

○ If children are involved, it can be helpful for them if the divorcing couple can light a parental candle from their now separate tapers, saying:

We kindle this lesser flame in affection and friendship, for we will always be united in the love of the children we created and nurtured together.

○ The children may want to add their tapers to the family flame, and this can be rekindled at family occasions when the divorced couple come together.

○ If there is bitterness, you can carry out the original ritual of separating the flame without the other person, and if you have children, use tapers representing you and your former partner to light a family candle. As you do this, you can ask that his or her heart may be softened and that you may still be as one in your love of the children.

It is very hard if the other person has acted callously and deserted you, is making matters hard financially or is manipulating the children. But if you can continue to carry out positive rituals, it will heal your own hurt and negative feelings – and even if the other person remains destructive, you and your children will benefit from your positive intent.

A ritual for **reconciliation**

After any reconciliation in a permanent relationship where there has been betrayal or separation, there can be a long period of doubt that can all too easily end in recriminations. A simple ceremony, repeated if necessary at regular intervals, can offer a unifying force. Some people use figure candles to represent the couple and I have seen lovely ones made from beeswax, but you may prefer to use either pink and green candles for love and reconciliation or, in the old alchemical tradition, silver for a female and gold for a male.

○ Surround the candles with pine needles for cleansing old angers and dried lavender for reviving love. Light your lover's candle and let him or her light yours, saying:

So do we rekindle love, passion, trust and fidelity.

○ Into your lover's flame sprinkle a few pine needles, saying:

Anger, resentment, bitterness, jealously, burn, burn away.

Your partner can carry out the same action in your flame.

○ Taking a few lavender flowers, sprinkle them in your partner's flame, saying:

Let wounds be healed by this gentle flower of comfort, harsh words spoken in haste or anger be unspoken in this herb of harmony, bad memories fade in the fragrance, leaving only good memories of the past and hopes for the future.

Your partner can do the same in your candle.

○ Sit quietly by the candlelight, hands joined, and as the candles burn down, rekindle the affection between you by recalling happy times before the parting and making plans and promises for the future.

○ Let the candles burn down naturally, and in the melting wax join your love together by inscribing a heart with your entwined initials. You can keep this as a special love token.

Candles for **bereavement**

Thousands and thousands of candles were burning in countless rows, some large, some medium-sized, others small. Every instant some were extinguished, and others again burnt up, so that the flames seemed to leap hither and thither in perpetual change. See, said Godfather Death, these are the lights of men's lives. The large ones belong to children, the medium-sized ones to married people in their prime, the little ones belong to old people, but children and young folks likewise have often only a tiny candle – one must go out before a new one is lighted.

FROM GODFATHER DEATH BROTHERS GRIMM

Giving validity to the symbolism of our life as a candle is the tradition of corpse-lights or candles. In many cultures and ages, people have seen lights circling the room as someone dies: these 'corpse candles' are said to be the soul leaving a body after death. Others have reported seeing a series of lights floating towards a dying person, and these are believed to be the essences of departed relatives coming to welcome the newly deceased person. Icelandic legends talk of fires burning on the top of ancient burial mounds where departed warriors are said to guard their treasure.

From the days when a body would remain at home until the funeral come many customs where the deceased is surrounded by flickering candles. Some

date back to old Jewish rituals, adopted by Christians, of lighting candles for the dead and dying. In Ireland, a corpse would be surrounded by 12 candles, while in the Scottish lowlands, when a body had been laid out, one of the oldest women present would circle the body three times with a 'sainting' or blessing candle and leave it burning all night.

Day of the Dead candle rituals

The modern Hallowe'en celebrations, with their plastic skeletons and ghost masks, are a poor relic of what was once a sacred period (called Samhain) for remembering and welcoming the dead to their family hearths. In Mexico, people still celebrate Hallowe'en in its traditional sense. El Dia del Muerte (the Day of the Dead) is All Souls' Day in the Catholic calendar. The feast is spread over two days: on 1 November departed children are remembered, and on 2 November the ghosts of adults are honoured. People in towns, cities and villages make a path with bright yellow flowers from the cemetery to their house, to guide the dead to their homes to visit them.

In Japan, at twilight on the evening of 13 August families make fires and burn incense in front of their homes. On the evening of 16 August they again make fires and burn incense at the gate to send off the souls for another year.

You may like to create a family candle festival at Hallowe'en.

- Light purple candles and place them on the family hearth or on a table near the natural focus of heat in the main living area.
- Decorate the bases of the candles with autumn greenery and a few evergreens as a reminder that life runs in a continuing cycle. Let the candlelight shine on any personal treasures of the departed.
- Prepare family meals that were favourites of the deceased relations and get out photographs of them.

A candle ritual on the anniversary of a loved one's death can express feelings too deep for words.

A private candle ritual
on the anniversary of a loved one's death

Graveyard vigils can be distressing, as it is hard to recall the essence of the person who has died and to hear their laughter in a place that has such sad memories of raw grief. But there is another way.

- On the anniversary of the death, spend time in places where you shared joyous memories, and at twilight kindle a special candle in the dead person's favourite colour or scented with their favourite fragrance.
- Look into the flame and speak words of love and any of regret that you would like to say if the person were present, and let the light be a link of love with the essential person you have lost, who lives on in their descendants and in all the kind deeds they performed and wise words they spoke. You may be rewarded with a sense of peace, perhaps a fleeting shadow, a touch as light as gossamer, a word softly spoken in your mind's ear or externally. Even if you did not use a scented candle, you may momentarily smell a fragrance associated with the loved one.
- When you have finished, blow out the candle, sit in the darkness for a while and shed any private tears, then either write a letter to or phone someone who may also be missing the person. Alternatively, you could make a gesture of friendship or help to a person or cause beloved by the deceased.

PART TWO

Beginning **Candle Magic**

CHAPTER FOUR

Candle Colours

Colour has played an important part in many magical systems for thousands of years, throughout the world, from the Babylonians and ancient Egyptians, to India and China. In modern magic, candle colours are a potent way of focusing the energies of a ritual towards a particular area of need or desire. They also contain the energies and vibrations inherent in each colour and their zodiacal associations.

Each colour is therefore a veritable powerhouse of stored symbolism. However, the important factor in your own colour work is consistency, and as you develop your own system you will find that certain colours naturally suggest themselves for definite purposes.

Use good-quality coloured candles that are the same colour all the way through (cheaper ones can be white inside under a thin, flaky layer of dye). There are great variations in colour associations and their meanings, so in the descriptions that follow below I have chosen examples where the different traditions agree.

White

White candles are used in protective, consecration and cleansing rituals, for healing the whole person, for spiritual matters, and for contact with one's higher self and angels or spirit guides. In magic, white represents light and clear vision, and so is helpful where a new beginning or a sudden burst of energy and enthusiasm is needed. White is a good colour for rites-of-passage work, especially for birth, marriage and welcoming rituals. White candles can also be substituted for any other colour.

Like silver, white is associated with female energies, lunar rituals and with the goddess and the moon – so a white candle is especially potent on Mondays, the day of the moon.

Use with diamonds, clear crystal quartz, zircon and pure white stones, especially those from the sea.

Gold

Gold is the colour of the sun and is associated with the solar deities, for example, the Egyptian Ra and the Roman Apollo. Golden candles are potent for worldly achievement, wealth and recognition, as well as long life. Use them for ambitious schemes and money-making rituals that require an instant or substantial return. Gold is also a colour for male/animus power, energy and change, and all rituals with noble or altruistic purpose. Candles of this colour are most potent on Sundays. Use them with amber, golden tiger's eye, topaz and citrine.

Silver

Silver is the colour of the moon and the moon goddesses, the Egyptian Isis and the Roman Diana. It is potent for all forms of divination (especially candle divination), for awakening clairvoyant, telepathic and psychometric abilities, for astral projection, and for rituals to invoke female/anima power, intuition and mysticism. It represents dreams, visions and a desire for fulfilment beyond the material world. In times of stress and sorrow, silver candles can remove negativity and promote inner stability.

The best day for silver candle rituals is Monday. Use with moonstones, whose colour deepens as the moon waxes, haematite, mother of pearl, snow and milky quartz, and rutilated quartz.

Red

Red is the colour of Mars, the god of war, and so is the colour of courage, determination, action, energy, sexual passion and potency. Red candles can be burned to increase the life force, for survival matters, physical health, strength and pleasure, willpower and also to rouse anger – not the petty anger of childish tantrums and spite, but the righteous anger that, if directed positively, can overcome injustice and bring about change. This is therefore a very powerful candle colour, and should be lit for worthy aims only and when you are in a positive frame of mind.

Red is the colour of the ancient element of fire. Its energies are male/animus and its candle rituals are best practised on a Tuesday.

Use with red agate, red jasper, obsidian, pyrites and garnets.

Orange

Orange is another solar colour, a colour of fertility, both physical and mental, of creativity and growth, for self-esteem and confidence, abundance of all kinds and independence.

Orange candle spells can also be used for career matters where creativity or dealing with people's needs are central. Above all, orange candle rituals are for joy and for the successful integration of all aspects of the personality into a harmonious whole.

Orange contains male/animus energies and its candle rituals are best performed on a Sunday.

Use with amber, orange agate, coral and carnelian.

Yellow

Yellow is the colour associated with Mercury, the Roman winged messenger of the gods. Through his skill and dexterity, he came to rule over commerce and medicine, and also became patron of tricksters and thieves. Yellow candles therefore encourage activity of all kinds, but especially mental exercise. Use them in rituals where you wish to gain another person's confidence and approval, or to win someone round in business or intellectual matters; to sharpen logic, improve memory and increase concentration; and for good luck on a journey. Yellow is also for careers in business, communication or the media.

As the colour of the ancient element of air, yellow is associated with male energies. Yellow candle rituals are most potent on a Wednesday.

Use with yellow jasper, topaz, yellow calcite and citrine.

Green

Candles in rainbow colours, each of which has unique energies that can be evoked in ritual.

Green is the colour of Venus, goddess of love, and is associated with candle rituals for love and for all matters where emotion, sympathy and empathy are required. It is also the colour of Mother Earth and so is potent for healing, for rites involving the natural world, herbs, gardening and tree magic, for growth and, by association, the growth of money in prosperity rituals. When green candles are used in rituals for wealth, they tend to encourage a gradual increase in profits or resources. As the fairy colour, they are also potent for spells for good luck.

Astrological *candle associations*

Each birth sun sign is represented by a colour or colours. There is disagreement about these associations, so I have given those mainly agreed upon. As long as you are consistent, you can go with these or other colours you find listed in different sources – or choose your special, favourite colour to act as your zodiacal candle.

An appropriately coloured candle can be lit in rituals to represent a person born in that period and at any time when you need to strengthen your confidence or identity. Each sun sign colour also represents a quality or strength and so can be burned if you need that quality in your life, even if it is not your own birth sign

colour. It is always most potent during its own sun period.

Aries (21 March–20 April): Red. *Courage*

Taurus (21 April–21 May): Pink. *Patience*

Gemini (22 May–21 June): Pale grey or yellow. *Versatility*

Cancer (22 June–22 July): Silver. *Hidden potential*

Leo (23 July–23 August): Gold or orange. *Power/energy*

Virgo (24 August–22 September): Green or pale blue. *Desire for perfection*

Libra (23 September–23 October): Blue or violet. *Balance*

Scorpio (24 October–22 November): Burgundy or red. *Insight*

Sagittarius (23 November–21 December): Yellow or orange. *Clear direction*

Capricorn (22 December–20 January): Brown or black. *Perseverance*

Aquarius (21 January–18 February): Indigo or dark blue. *Independence*

Pisces (19 February–20 March): White or mauve. *Intuition*

Green has female/anima energies, and Friday is the day of the week when green candle rites work best.

Use with jade, malachite, olivine/peridot, emerald and cat's eye.

Blue

Blue is the 'healing colour' and is associated with Jupiter and other father/sky gods such as the Viking Odin, in their role as law-givers and powerful rulers. In magic, blue can expand the boundaries of possibility, and create confidence and power mingled with altruism and idealism. Burn a blue candle when principles are at stake, to discover the truth and receive guidance, when dealing with officialdom and when seeking justice.

Blue candles can be lit for the expansion of mental horizons, for success and the increase of possibility. They also represent the expansion of physical horizons and travel. Above all, blue offers protection and calm in the midst of times of crisis and turmoil.

Blue is the colour of the ancient element of water and contains male/animus energies. Its day is Thursday.

Use with sodalite, lapis lazuli, sapphire, blue lace agate and turquoise.

Purple

Purple, like blue, is associated with Jupiter, but represents the wise teacher and keeper of hidden, unconscious wisdom. In magic, purple candle rituals provide a link with higher dimensions and can bring happiness to all who yearn for something beyond the material plane.

Purple candles aid meditation, past-life work, candle and mirror scrying (divination), and astral travel, and are good for psychic protection and for the prevention of nightmares. Purple candles can also be used for all rituals where the facts are not clear, for matters of secrecy, for healing the spirit and banishing what lies in the past but is still haunting the present, and for remembering departed loved ones.

Purple's energies are male/animus and the best day for purple candle rituals is Thursday.

Use with amethyst, sugilite, sodalite, peacock's eye (bornite) and purple kunzite.

Pink

Pink is a colour associated with Venus, the goddess of love, so pink candle rituals are excellent for matters involving the gentler aspects of love, romance, affection and friendship, the healing of wounded emotions, for quiet sleep and for the mending of quarrels. They can also be used for all family matters, for the rekindling of trust and for new relationships. Pink candle rituals will help to attract new friends and lovers.

Pink is associated with female/anima energies and all female rituals, and its day is Friday.

Use with pink kunzite, rose quartz, tourmaline and coral.

Brown

Brown candles need not be dull. Like a ploughed field in the autumn sun, their colours can range from a pale fawn to a rich rust or deep golden brown. Brown comes under the auspices of Saturn, Old Father Time, the god of fate and the passage of time.

Brown can be used in rituals to locate lost objects, and for anything to do with the home, older people, practical matters and pets. As brown is another colour of Mother Earth, brown candles can act as grounding, balance and protection, giving ideas firm foundations, bringing success through hard work, and for money or material and financial security. Brown is a nurturing colour and is the natural focus of maternal matters, instincts, and acceptance of others with faults and weaknesses.

Brown energies can be male/animus for Saturn or female/anima for Mother Earth, according to the nature of the ritual; these are best performed on Saturdays.

Use with tiger's eye, fossilized wood, brown and banded agates, and brown jasper.

Grey

Grey candles are used for all spells to create an aura of invisibility before going into a potentially threatening or confrontational situation, and for smoothing down potential conflict. Grey is also the colour for reaching compromises and erasing negative feelings.

These candles are under the auspices of Jupiter and Saturn, but emit neutral energies and can be used on any day when needed.

Use with smoky quartz, banded grey agate or a grey pebble from the beach.

Black

Many people do not like using black candles because of their associations with black magic. If you feel that these associations are too strong for you, substitute dark blue, dark purple or brown candles in rituals. However, black candles, which are ruled by Saturn, can be potent in all forms of banishing magic, for leaving behind old sorrows and redundant relationships, for acknowledging grief and for rituals of parting.

In a positive sense, black – like brown – is the colour of acceptance, whether of a restriction or of the frailties of self and others, and so it is a candle colour of forgiveness.

Black is another earth colour, containing both male and female energies. Rituals using these candles are best practised on a Saturday.

Use with obsidian, jet or black onyx.

Using candle colours in **rituals**

The first factor to consider is the purpose for which the ritual is being performed. If this need involves two related factors, you can include two candles or a candle that blends the two colours. For example, if you wanted to pursue a career which involved both caring for people and travel, you could use an orange candle (remember, orange candle spells can also be used for career matters where creativity or dealing with people's needs are central) and blue for travel, lighting them in the order of their importance to you.

The next consideration is whom the ritual is for. Some practitioners do not light a candle to represent the self; however, if the need involves you and another person, it may be helpful to light your own zodiacal candle first and then, if you know their birth date, the sun sign candle of the other person.

If in doubt, you can substitute a white or beeswax candle. Use brown for a pet, pink for a child, and in love rituals use green for yourself and pink for a lover or potential lover, or vice versa. If sex is the prime mover, red may be more appropriate, perhaps counterbalanced by a spiritual purple. For someone who is ill and absent, light a purple or pink candle.

You can add as many candles as you wish, as long as you designate a purpose or person for each.

Candle **healing**

The Babylonians called the healing power of light the 'medicine of the gods'. Healing colours have been used for thousands of years in China, by the ancient Egyptians and in Indian Ayurvedic medicine. Although candle colour healing is more recent, the use of beeswax candles as a source of healing light is traditional.

I am not suggesting for a moment that in cases of illness you should put your faith entirely in candles. This type of healing is *complementary* – an additional boost to whatever type of medicine or care is recommended. Whether its effects are purely psychological or due to some power that modern science cannot explain, I and many others have found the effects beneficial.

Candle colour healing is very gentle, using either crystals or mirrors to amplify the light or candles anointed with fragranced virgin olive oil. You can also use scented coloured candles, for example lavender and rose, which are soothing for many ills (see Chapter 5). Candlelight is especially good for healing children, older people and anyone who is feeling vulnerable or anxious.

The act of extinguishing the flame enables the healing energies to be directed to absent friends or relations who are sick or troubled, and is also good for healing people for whom physical contact would not be appropriate.

Performing candle healing

○ Choose a candle related to the disorder, or use white or beeswax for any illness or stress. Anoint your candle with fragranced olive oil (see Chapter 5), and as you do so visualize golden light entering the candle from the cosmos.

A colour candle ritual for **increasing prosperity**

This ritual uses a single tall, green beeswax candle for the gradual growth of prosperity – a suitable occasion for carrying out this ritual might be the launch of a business venture or project. If you need money for an immediate crisis, substitute a gold candle. If possible, begin on a waxing moon soon after dusk.

You can buy green beeswax candles or, better still, make your own, endowing their creation with all your hopes for increasing money flow.

I have also carried out this ritual with an undyed yellow beeswax candle for a faster flow of money.

- Soften the wax of the candle very slightly near the base and press a coin into the soft wax. Any coin will do, but for a new business you can follow the old trading principle called 'handsel'. This involves keeping the first coin you are given towards your venture, preferably on a Monday or on New Year's Day.
- Dress the candle with one of the oils of prosperity: cinnamon, mint, patchouli, pine or cloves (see also Chapter 5). You can use one of the special candle-anointing oils or a small quantity of virgin olive oil in which a single drop of one of the money oils has been diluted.
- Rub the candle in clockwise circles, first from the centre downwards and then from the centre upwards, ending at the place where you will light the candle. As you rub in the oil, visualize money flowing to you as a stream that increases in width and intensity.
- Place your hands momentarily around the candle to form a physical link between you and the symbol of your need. Light your green money candle, saying:

Candle glow,
Money flow,
Prospects grow.

- Place a single coin and a green crystal – such as aventurine, jade, peridot or a glass nugget – to the north of the candle to form the beginning of a circle and blow out the candle.
- At the same time the next evening, relight your candle and repeat the chant, adding another coin and crystal to the circle in a clockwise direction. Sit for a few minutes in the candlelight, visualizing your plans bearing fruit, and you may find ideas come to you. Blow out the candle.
- Continue the ritual each evening, adding coins and crystals, until the candle coin falls out or the candle has burned too low to relight. On this last night, space the coins and crystals if the circle is incomplete, so that they form a complete circle around the candle, using the fallen coin as the last in the circle.
- If the venture is ongoing, you can repeat the ritual on each waxing moon, reusing the coins and crystals, which you can keep in a special green box or cloth bag. Between rituals, keep your handsel coin with your account books or in a tiny bag in your wallet or purse. Place your handsel in the new candle.

- If the sick person is not with you, you may wish to use a photograph of them or make a 'poppet' – a featureless doll in the appropriate colour, filled with healing herbs such as chamomile, elder flowers, lavender, mint, rosemary or vervain. Tie a ribbon of the same colour around the afflicted part on the doll, or around the head of the doll if it is a whole-body disorder or an affliction of the mind or spirit.
- Light the candle and circle it nine times anti-clockwise over the photograph or doll to remove any pain or anxiety, and nine times clockwise to insert feelings of calm or energy.

Place the candle behind the symbol and visualize the coloured light entering the person who is sick or distressed.
- When you are ready, blow out the candle, saying:

Go light to where you are most needed and bring health and healing to
[name] if he/she will accept it.

Healing properties of **candle colours**

White or undyed candles, for example of beeswax, can form a focus for all forms of healing since white is the synthesis of all other colours. This promotes health and healing, and integration of mind, body and soul. White light is a natural pain reliever, and can help to protect against cerebral disorders, to increase breast milk in nursing mothers, speed the mending of broken bones and relieve calcium deficiency and toothache.

Gold candles are especially potent for overcoming addictions, obsessions and compulsions, and for relieving depression. Gold is the most powerful healing colour of all, associated with long life and immortality.

Red candles are natural restorers of energy levels, good for raising blood pressure and improving circulation, and promoting cellular growth and activity; they are used in healing blood ailments, especially anaemia. Red light is linked to reproduction and fertility and relieves sexual dysfunction, especially impotence; it also helps with pains in the feet, hands and bones.

Orange is another colour of energy and warmth, easing arthritis and rheumatism, and is used for increasing the pulse rate, relieving gall bladder and kidney problems and stones, menstrual and muscle cramps and allergies, and lifting exhaustion. Orange also strengthens the immune system.

Yellow stimulates the nervous system, improving memory and concentration and easing eczema and skin problems; it also promotes a healthy metabolism, and calms anxiety and stress-related ailments that may affect the digestive system adversely.

Green candles lower high blood pressure, being a restorative for the heart, lungs and respiratory system, and fight infections and viruses, especially influenza, bronchitis, fevers and colds. They also counter panic attacks, addictions and food-related illnesses. Green is a good healing colour because it stimulates tissue and cell growth and general body regeneration.

Blue is called the healing colour because a blue aura is often seen around healers. It is a natural antiseptic, soothing and cooling, relieving burns, cuts, bruises, insomnia, inflammation of the skin and mouth, sore throats and childhood rashes and teething pains; blue also lowers high temperatures and high blood pressure. All shades of blue, such as violet and indigo, are helpful in reducing migraines and headaches.

Violet and indigo are cleansing and uplifting, counteracting doubts and negativity. Violet candles can be burned for treating allergies, asthma, sleep disorders and stress-related illnesses. Indigo helps to ease eye, ear, nose and skin problems and migraines, and soothes the nervous system. It aids the healing of deep tissue and bones, and is a natural sedative.

Rose/pink is the gentle healer, promoting restful sleep and pleasant dreams and encouraging optimism. Ear, eye and gland problems, head pains and psychosomatic illnesses fall under its auspices, as do all disorders relating to children and babies, especially fretfulness and hyperactivity.

○ Sit quietly in the darkness, letting your love follow the light to the sufferer.

○ You can carry out this ritual for someone who is present if they sit on the opposite side of the candle to you. Ask the person to visualize with you the light from the candle entering a point of pain and spiralling round their body, gently dispersing the discomfort. Say words such as:

> *Candle light, candle bright,*
> *Shed on [the person you are trying to help]*
> *Your golden light.*
> *Disperse pain, make whole again,*
> *Discord ease, fill with peace.*

○ As you blow out the candle, direct the coloured light to yourself or to enter the person to be healed.

Light reflected through a crystal sphere amplifies the body's own healing energies.

A crystal or mirror *healing candle ritual*

Crystal balls are traditionally used for healing by focusing sunlight through the sphere towards a sick person or body part, being careful not to attract too much heat in the glass. The light from candles is equally potent when reflected through a crystal sphere, a mirror or an agate egg, especially for chronic conditions or anxieties, or for gradual healing.

○ Choose appropriately coloured candles and make a semi-circle of light so that they reflect within the shiny surface of the sphere or mirror. Do not look at the candle flames directly but at the reflected light, and visualize the pain, distress or lack of energy moving from you into the glowing surface. Say:

Fade with the light from here, pain/sorrow/weakness, be absorbed, contained, diminished, a pale reflection, soon to cease.

○ Blow out all the candles at once if you can or rapidly in succession, saying:

Be gone pain, fade, banished into darkness, gone from the body into the glass.

○ Sprinkle the sphere or mirror with a few rose petals, waft over it a cleansing incense such as pine or cedar, and let a single drop of pure spring water fall on to the surface of the sphere or mirror.

○ Rub the sphere or mirror with a soft, dark cloth until it sparkles again. Wrap it in another lighter-coloured cloth and place it on top of a high cupboard or in a drawer until it is needed again. Wash the dark cloth and hang it in the fresh air to dry.

○ You can repeat this ritual as often as you need.

CHAPTER FIVE

Candle Fragrances

Candle fragrances offer a method of endowing individual candles with additional significance in rituals and psychic work. Herbs, flowers, oils and spices have magical as well as healing associations, and these are listed below. You do not need to anoint a candle for every ritual – just when you are carrying out a more formal ceremony or feel you need to concentrate especially hard because the goal is urgent or perhaps more difficult to attain.

You can anoint or dress candles with scented oil, or use candles that have fragrance already added. When you do anoint candles with oils, they become

Herbs and spices, fruits and flowers

Allspice Brings money, love and healing, and can add warmth and abundance to festivities, especially Christmas and New Year.

Apple The old Druidic love and marriage symbol represents love, fidelity and marriage. Aids general health, youthfulness and fertility, and love divination.

Basil Attracts and keeps love true, draws money through endeavour, aids astral projection, deters negativity, and banishes nervous tension, insomnia and also tiredness when it is not possible to sleep.

Bayberry Popular among the early American settlers, bayberry brings luck and prosperity to a house in which it is burned. Used at Christmas and New Year especially, it weakens destructive influences.

Bergamot Potent for matters concerning money and property. Bergamot is a natural purifier and lifts depression, releasing inner potential and hidden talents.

Cedar Another natural purifier of body, mind and spirit, cedar removes all negativity and promotes optimism, relieving stress and helping with nervous conditions that may appear as physical illnesses; it is associated with oratory and its powers improve communication skills.

Chamomile Gentle and soothing, used for all health and magical matters relating to children and babies. Good for inducing sleep and calm in people of all ages, for bringing peace and harmony, and for repelling unwelcome visitors.

Cinnamon A natural stimulant for clairvoyance and psychic awareness, which promotes concentration and is potent in money rituals and also to draw success. Traditionally used to anoint candles for love and sex rituals.

Citronella A protective fragrance, it magically draws boundaries around the self against the intrusion of others, and repels physical negativity and those who unwittingly drain energies.

Cloves Another money fragrance, improving memory, warming and stimulating to the system, cloves turn away gossip, malice and envy. A natural aphrodisiac, they both attract love and awaken sexual desire.

Eucalyptus Promotes adaptability, increases energy and power, and heals mind, body and spirit of any pain, depression or illness. Relieves mental and physical congestion and purifies a home after quarrels.

Frankincense One of the three gifts of the Magi, it brings courage, good fortune and prosperity of all kinds, especially of the spirit; banishes compulsions, obsessions and destructive habits; aids concentration and dispels all forms of negativity and threat; helps in astral projection. Frankincense is often used in more formal magic.

Geranium Offers harmony of mind, body and spirit, redressing any imbalance naturally, and so can act as either soother or uplifter, according to the user's mood. Geranium can calm nervous tension and depression, and clear away doubt; it brings acceptance of human weakness, affection, romance and gentle love.

Ginger Aids potency and brings long life. Called the 'universal healer' in the Indian Ayurvedic tradition, ginger attracts money and success and endows energy for any endeavour.

more flammable, so you need to be extra-cautious about sparks. For safety, it is best to use a fireproof tray beneath your candlesticks.

The following herbs, oils and spices can be purchased relatively easily as scented candles or night lights: many supermarkets and manufacturers of air fresheners have branched out into quite exotic candle fragrances. You can also buy or make anointing oils and doing so will personalize your candle by endowing it with your own individual hopes, fears and dreams.

If you are making your own candles, you can buy special oil-soluble perfumes from craft shops for mixing into the wax before it is put into the mould. But if you do not have the time or facilities for candle-making then the easiest way to create a scented candle is to add two or three drops of scented oil around the burning wick of a plain candle using an eye dropper, being careful not to drop the oil into the flame. This can give a potent fragrance, albeit for a short time.

Heather Brings luck and is a symbol of devotion; used in rain magic when burned, heather is also a fertility symbol.

Heliotrope Improves clairvoyance, psychic powers and meditation, and encourages psychic invisibility if you are going into a confrontational situation where you need to keep a low profile. Heliotrope offers protection from all danger, especially physical harm.

Honeysuckle Increases intuition and psychic awareness; brings prosperity and helps to maintain it, as well as healing and protection.

Jasmine For rituals of love, passion and creativity, jasmine cleanses the aura and offers protection.

Juniper Traditionally burned in homes in Scotland at New Year to purify the house from the negative influences of the Old Year. Juniper also increases psychic awareness, offering protection and increasing male potency.

Lavender The fragrance of gentleness, for attracting love and acceptance of human frailty, it reduces all forms of stress and anxiety, dispels cruelty (especially in lovers), and brings peace, reconciliation and healing after

betrayal in love. Also for wishes of all kinds and to bring sleep to insomniacs and those who suffer from nightmares, lavender is another fragrance for children and babies.

Lemon Brings clarity of thought and cuts through indecision; lemon brings protection, not least from illusion.

Lilac A fragrance for happy memories, past-life recall, and protection for loved ones. Lilac brings benign influence and helps with decision-making.

Mint For travel, money and house moves, driving away illness and negativity; for prophetic dreams.

Musk The passion-bringer, for fertility and sex magic; also for confidence, self-esteem and strength.

Myrrh The healer of pain, bringing wisdom through experience; a natural protector, myrrh brings peace and spiritual awareness. Good for meditation and visualization, myrrh is also used in more formal magic, often combined with frankincense.

Orange For confidence, rejuvenation, harmony, energy, power and purification.

Pine The cleanser, assisting change and transformation. For money, healing, speaking true, illumination and knowing the truth, pine ends

pointless resentment and feelings of hostility.

Rose For attracting love, unconditional love, fidelity, forgiveness, harmony and peace. Brings together lovers and friends; for relationships of all kinds.

Rosewood For reconciliation and harmony of mind, body and spirit; good if unsettling issues are to be discussed or after any conflict.

Sage For wisdom and cleansing, long life and health, divination and meditation, bringing visions of past and future. Sage offers protection from all forms of harm and negative feelings in self and others.

Sandalwood For balance, soothing fears and also relieving depression and nervous tension. It also acts as an aphrodisiac and is used for love and sex magic, for healing and for increasing psychic awareness.

Sweetgrass In the Native American tradition sweetgrass connects with the world of spirit, calling down health and plenty from the benign forces above as it burns. It also aids change and transformation.

Vanilla For energy, happiness and good fortune of all kinds; also for love and sex magic. Vanilla aids mental powers.

Making fragrant **candle oils**

Candle-anointing oils are available in many fragrances and often their names will indicate their purpose. Find out what the ingredients are, as those made with herbs, flowers and essential oils tend to be gentler and induce a more delicate fragrance than synthetic products. However, making your own oil can help to focus your mind on the purpose for which you wish to use it. The following are two of the more popular methods.

The sun infusion method

You can use either dried or fresh herbs and flowers. This method takes several weeks, but at stages throughout its creation you can focus on your need and visualize its fruition, adding a simple chant to endow it with power, for example:

> *Rose, rose bring me love*

or

> *Mint, mint, send me money.*

The more personalized the ingredients, the more potent the oil, so if you can use mint or roses from the garden these will further endow the fragrance with your essence.

A CANDLE OIL FOR LOVE USING THE SUN INFUSION METHOD

To make a candle-anointing oil for love, use a good quality virgin olive oil and richly scented damask rose petals if possible, although any red rose petals can be substituted.

- Fill a large jar or bottle with oil and add rose petals so that they are smothered with oil but not too tightly packed. Cover with an airtight lid and leave in direct sunlight.
- As the petals turn brown, remove them and add fresh ones. Continue until the oil turns slightly pink. This may take 20 or more changes of petals during the summer in a cooler climate, but it is the best method of all for capturing the essence and fragrance of the roses.
- Strain out the roses through cheesecloth or muslin, being careful to squeeze out any oil from the petals. Some people leave the rose petals in the jar – this is a matter of personal preference.

A faster candle oil infusion method

- Fill a jar or wide-necked bottle three-quarters full with freshly gathered rose petals. Slowly pour in the oil to cover the petals and fill the jar or bottle.
- Seal with an airtight lid and leave to stand for four days, inverting it every 24 hours before returning it to its original position.
- After four days, take a second jar and fill that three-quarters full with freshly gathered rose petals. Strain the oil from the first jar through a piece of muslin or cheesecloth, remembering to squeeze the oil from the discarded petals. Add the oil to the new jar and seal it with an airtight lid, again leaving it to stand for four days, turning the jar every day.
- Continue this process for two weeks and then, if you wish, strain the jar of rose oil to remove the browning petals.

For either method, store the oil in amber or dark-coloured bottles. If you are using dried herbs or flowers you will need less, about three-quarters the amount of fresh herbs.

The fragrances of herbs and flowers traditionally carry associations of love, healing, peace and protection.

Anointing *candles with oil*

You can use fragranced virgin olive oil for dressing candles for any purpose. Some people add a pinch of salt for its purifying and life-giving properties.

- Before beginning, pour a small quantity of the oil into a clear glass or ceramic dish and gently swirl it nine times clockwise with a ceramic or glass spoon, visualizing light pouring into it and endowing it with healing and magical energies.
- Use a previously unlit candle, as this will not have absorbed any energies apart from those with which you endow it. Rub the oil into the candle in an upwards motion, starting in the middle of the candle. Rub only in that direction, concentrating on the purpose of your ritual. You need use only a small quantity

of oil as the action is symbolic. See the qualities of your oil entering the candle.

- Then, starting in the middle again, rub the candle downwards, concentrating on your goal. A few practitioners will rub from base to top for attracting magic and from top to bottom for banishing magic. In such cases they usually use a white candle for attracting energies and a black for banishing.
- By physically touching the candle with the oil, it is said that you are charging the candle with your personal vibrations, so that when it is lit, it becomes an extension of your mental power and life energy. If the candle represents another person and they are present, ask them to anoint their own candle.
- If you light a candle on successive days, you should re-anoint it each time if the ritual is a formal one (see Chapter 7), visualizing the partial completion of the goal.

Sally's lavender oil candle ritual *for overcoming insomnia*

Sally is a single parent with teenage children, who had recently lost a valuable contract in her freelance office bureau. She had been lying awake at night worrying about money and her children, who were into the usual teenage rebellions and refusing to help around the house. Because she could not sleep, Sally was unable to concentrate during the day and felt increasingly powerless. With multiple problems, it can sometimes be best to begin with the one that, if resolved, will release energy to tackle the others. If Sally were not so tired, she could bid for other contracts and be more assertive with her children. She decided to tackle her problem with a candle-dressing ritual rather than pills.

- Sally made lavender oil by the faster infusion method, using lavender from her garden. At each stage of turning the jar and replacing the flowers, she repeated:

  Lavender bring me quiet sleep, that I may wake renewed.

To Sally's surprise, she fell asleep more easily as the oil infused and she endowed it with her need for harmony, although she still woke long before dawn.

- Sally chose a large pink candle, the colour for peace of mind, and anointed it with her lavender oil about half an hour before bedtime on the waning moon, to take away her sleeplessness. As she rubbed the oil into the candle, she repeated the chant she had used in making the oil.
- Sally lit the candle and saw herself floating on soft purple clouds, fragranced with lavender. She blew out the candle just before she went to sleep and slept an extra hour, waking only once in the night.
- Sally continued to light her pink candle on six further consecutive nights, anointing it each time and repeating her chant. On the final night she sat while it burned away, taking her insomnia with it. By the seventh night, Sally was sleeping much better and is now negotiating several new contracts.

Endowing Candles with Power

Candle wish magic is a good way of focusing on what it is you actually want. Many wishes we make are quite vague:

I would like to be richer/better-looking/happier.

But if you can focus on a realistic, specific initial need and break down a long-term goal into smaller, manageable steps with an approximate timescale, then it will be easier to fulfil your aim, both in magical terms and in the action that must inevitably follow in the everyday world if you are really to succeed.

It is also important to be sure that what you ask for is what you really want. I have a good friend who is intelligent, beautiful and witty, but whose most powerful wish is to get married. She can picture the dress, the ceremony and the music, but is vague about the relationship that goes with the trimmings – and sometimes this can lead her into less than suitable choices of potential partners.

So do you really want a partner, whatever the cost? Do you really want never to have to work again? The folk tales tell us with more than a grain of truth that we must be careful what we wish for, because our wishes may be granted in a way that we do not really want.

For example, I once wanted so desperately to go to the United States that I carried out a wish ceremony, asking to get there any way, anyhow. Shortly afterwards I was offered the chance to take part in a television show in Los Angeles, all expenses paid. However, my visit was interrupted by the Los Angeles earthquake of January 1994, and as I was staying close to the epicentre, the results were quite devastating.

You should also ask yourself:

Can I make this candle wish without interfering with anyone else's free will or happiness?

The best magic practitioners make only positive affirmations, unless they are ridding themselves of a destructive habit or relationship – and then they aim for banishing the negative influence rather than the person.

When you are making your wish, do not be afraid to ask for something material, because if you are constantly worried about money or security it can block your natural psychic energies. We all have earthly needs and meeting these is a vital part of our existence as evolving spiritual beings. If you need several hundred pounds for urgent repairs on your car, want to take your family on holiday or need a break yourself, ask for that.

If you practise defining the conditions and parameters of candle wishes, when you then come to inscribe a candle with a single word to represent your need, such as 'love' or 'attraction', you can mentally endow it with a carefully structured thought that will soar away like a well-aimed arrow to hit the right target.

Emotion and need are also important. If you have only a vague notion that you might like to move house, a candle wish or any other kind of ritual is unlikely to succeed. Focus is as important in magic as it is in all walks of life. Therefore, the process of preparation can be quite illuminating, because sometimes what we think matters is, under scrutiny, not so important.

Burning candle wishes

Burning candle wishes is a very ancient form of candle magic in which your desires are consigned to the cosmos in the candle flame.

- Begin by writing your wish on a thin piece of paper about 23cm (9in) long, in the colour of the candle you are going to burn or on pure white paper. You may decide to use a magical alphabet, and on pages 50–6 I have provided two that carry additional significance in each letter.
- As you write, visualize yourself getting your promotion, sitting on the beach under a palm tree, or doing whatever it is that you desire. Create the scene in your imagination – a practitioner's most powerful tool – in as much detail as possible; fill out the picture with sounds, scents and touch so that you can hear the sea crashing on the shores of the Mediterranean or feel the smooth leather of the seats of your new car.
- When you have finished, fold up the paper into a taper shape narrowed at one end and, if you want, add your birth sign symbol (see Chapter 6) to the front.
- Use a large candle in a colour that corresponds with your need (see Chapter 4) and place a large fireproof plate or tray underneath it. Hold the narrowed end of the paper downwards in the candle flame and set light to it. As you look into the flame, visualize whatever it is that you most need or desire moving closer to. Anticipate the pleasure, excitement or relief the fulfilment of your wish will bring, and visualize alternative scenarios of the source or the steps you will take to that fulfilment. Let the paper burn away on the fireproof tray.
- When you light the paper, if it ignites instantly and burns steadily, then your aim will be swiftly accomplished. If your taper goes out, light it again: I have had to make three or more in an attempt for a new venture to take off. If it burns slowly, stops, smoulders and begins again, you will succeed – it just takes longer. As your taper burns, look into the candle flame and visualize yourself happier and more successful, but still the you that you are now.
- Leave the candle to burn away in a safe place. When it is finished, see if the melted wax has formed an image. This may contain a significant message about your wish (see Chapter 13).
- Tip the ash that is left on to plain white paper and, holding the paper firmly in both hands, gently shake the ashes until they form a picture. If you do not have enough, burn a second blank taper of the same colour in the flame. You may see a picture or several images as you would in tea-leaf reading: perhaps an animal, a bird, a person. The first interpretation of the image that comes into

OPPOSITE Strengthen the power of a candle wish by writing the wish in an ancient runic alphabet.

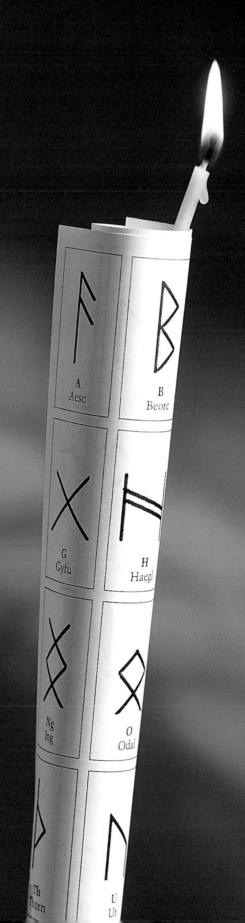

Sending the ashes to the four winds

If your wish is very urgent or vital to future survival, go to the top of a hill and hold up a scarf to determine the way the wind is blowing. The wind direction is assessed according to the direction from which it flows, so that a scarf that is streaming east is being driven by the west wind. Each of the winds from the four cardinal points – North, East, South and West – is associated with different energies.

East winds are associated with new beginnings and a fresh approach to old problems, with clear communication, change, logic and open-mindedness.

South winds are associated with rapid growth, blossoming and development, and with the power of swift, decisive action to resolve problems and crises.

West winds are linked with the fruition of dreams, resolving issues and also accepting what cannot be resolved.

North winds are linked with harmony and intuitive powers.

Scatter your ashes in the blowing wind, accepting which energy is paramount at the time you make your wish.

your mind will be the right one. You may find that the symbol is one that appears in your dreams or will appear very shortly afterwards.

○ If you use your wish candle for divination by dripping wax on to paper (see Chapter 13), you can add the ash to the wax and create a whole scene. This can be a very effective form of divination if your wish is concerned with a major change or the immediate future is uncertain.

Inscribing *candles*

Carving your wishes and intentions into a candle endows it with your special energies, and as you etch each letter or symbol these energies become concentrated.

If you anoint a candle (see Chapter 5), engrave it afterwards, although you may feel that inscribing it is sufficient. Given a light touch, it is not difficult to engrave candles using a pin, a nail or an awl.

Making an awl

The awl is the traditional magical tool used to engrave candles with names or properties. It is a small engraving tool, about the size of a pencil or pen, with a fine, rounded end, and you can buy one from craft or even hardware stores as well as New Age outlets. If you can obtain one of the old-fashioned wooden pens with a nib on the end, that is equally good. You can also use a cartridge pen without any ink in it, in which case choose a gold colour for the sun or silver for the moon, and keep it just for marking candles.

Alternatively, you may prefer to make your own awl to imbue it with your personal vibrations.

○ Select a piece of wood, perhaps hazel for wisdom or ash for healing and the expansion of possibilities, and carve it into shape, or use a sturdy twig of the right shape.

○ Tap a small nail into the narrower end of the wood, being very careful not to split it.

○ With a pair of sharp cutters, remove the head of the nail and sharpen the point against a stone, visualizing golden energies pouring into it from the cosmos and the rich rust light from the earth.

Personalize your awl (whether bought or made) by painting or etching your name on it, along with your astrological birth sign or some magical symbols.

Consecrate your engraving tool by sprinkling sea salt over it, passing it nine times anti-clockwise through an incense stick of frankincense or myrrh – which are natural cleansers – circling it nine times clockwise over a candle flame and finally sprinkling it with spring water that has been left in a crystal or glass bowl for a day and night cycle.

Engraving your candle

If you decide to engrave your candle, you can write just an initial for a person's name or your wish on it. I have chosen two alphabets that are especially adaptable for engraving purposes, since they are based entirely on straight lines. If a letter you need is not included, use either an approximation of the sound or miss it out: these alphabets are not meant as exact correspondences. The runic script was used for inscriptions and magical intentions in the Viking and Anglo-Saxon worlds, while the Druidic tree alphabet was originally for divination and was signed on the hands of the Druids as they carried their wisdom in secret after they were driven out of their last British stronghold of Anglesey by the Romans. Other magical alphabets include the Theban, Egyptian hieroglyphics and the Angelic

As a candle is engraved with a tree stave, it absorbs the hopes and dreams of the inscriber.

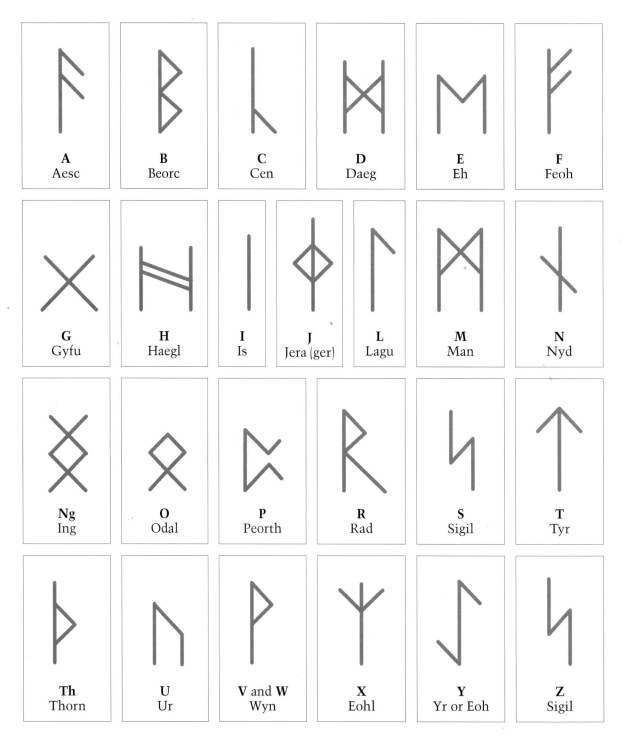

A Aesc	**B** Beorc	**C** Cen	**D** Daeg	**E** Eh	**F** Feoh
G Gyfu	**H** Haegl	**I** Is	**J** Jera (ger)	**L** Lagu	**M** Man	**N** Nyd
Ng Ing	**O** Odal	**P** Peorth	**R** Rad	**S** Sigil	**T** Tyr
Th Thorn	**U** Ur	**V** and **W** Wyn	**X** Eohl	**Y** Yr or Eoh	**Z** Sigil

For example, my name, Cassandra, would be spelt:

scripts, and some of the books suggested in the Further Reading section will help you with these.

Whether you are writing a wish or an intention, the power of an ancient, lost language forms a transition between the everyday world, where magic is necessarily grounded, and the sphere of the spirit, using the accumulated wisdom of centuries or even millennia past.

The name of a person or the wish is traditionally etched on to the candle from the wick end to the base. On the other side of the candle you can, if you wish, add astrological and planetary signs (see page 57).

Runic writing

Rune means 'secret' or 'hidden', from the word *ru* of the ancient Northern European languages. Runes were angular markings made by the Germanic races (the English, German and Scandinavian peoples who shared a common heritage and language that gradually split into different dialects).

The runic symbols (see opposite) were more than just an alphabet: each symbolized a whole concept, much like a Tarot card. The runes have a meaning hidden in each letter, a power that has been lost in modern scripts where, for example, A is a sound or letter but has no symbolism in itself. Therefore every time you write your name or a wish in runic you are adding the potency of each letter meaning, not in a frightening way but as a focus for your own power.

For each letter I have given the meaning of the symbol, so that you can see how what you write can focus different energies. You can also write a single runic symbol to invoke its individual power.

Practise writing your name and simple messages. Because the system isn't sufficiently complex to match English spellings with all their variations, you may end up compromising. What matters is the essence of the message.

You will find that some tree names – for example, birch, ash and yew – appear in both this and the tree alphabet, so that if you are adding a symbol of power to your candle you can inscribe both runic and Ogham symbols, perhaps overlapping. This redoubles the power. Generally, you should use only one magical alphabet in a wish, but where you are using single but complementary symbols this rule does not apply.

Aesc A is the ash tree, symbol of strength, endurance and wisdom, for the world tree Yggdrassil that supported the nine worlds of Norse cosmology was made of ash (see also Nuinn, the ash in the tree staves). Use this symbol on candles to give power for long-term goals.

Beorc B is the birch tree, symbol of the Mother Goddess and, because of its association with the birch trees that covered Norway after the end of the last Ice Age, of rebirth and new beginnings (see also Beith, the birch in the tree staves). Engrave this on your candles if you are trying to rebuild an aspect of your life or are starting a new venture.

Cen C (also **K** and **ch**) is the torch, one of the fire runes, that was used to light the dark halls of the Vikings during the long winter nights, so it has come to represent the inner voice and flame. Use this for rituals where you are seeking to build up your self-confidence and resist the pressures of others (see also Ailm, the fir/pine in the tree staves).

Daeg D is the dawn, the awakening, enlightenment, light at the end of the tunnel, and is named after Daeg, son of Nott, goddess of night, whose radiance was so dazzling that the gods fashioned him a chariot drawn by a pure white horse, Skin-Faxi ('shining mane'), from whom also emanated sparkling light. Draw this on your candle if you have been going through a difficult patch or are depressed.

Eh E is the horse, symbol of harmony between rider and man. So beloved were warriors' horses that they were given elaborate burials when they died. Odin the Viking Father God (Woden to the Anglo-Saxons) had an eight-legged steed, Sleipnir, who had magical runes engraved on his teeth. Use this symbol when you need harmony either within or among family, friends or colleagues.

Feoh F represented the cattle that the travelling peoples took with them on their conquests, and so came to represent wealth and the price that must be paid for any choice. Carve this rune on your candle when money is an issue or if you have to calculate the consequences of change or a decision.

Gyfu G is the gift or giving, which also represented relationships, especially sexual ones, and so is one of the fertility runes. Use this rune on your candle for fertility and marriage spells.

Haegl H is one of the protective runes and was the mother or core rune, representative of the cosmic seed or grain of life. It stood for facing hardships in order to move forward. Etch the Haegl rune if your ritual is for overcoming difficulties or you are facing disruption in your life.

Is I is the rune of ice, a rune that represents waiting for the ice to melt and the right moment to come. Use this rune on candles to clear stagnation of any kind.

Jera (or **Ger**) **J** is the harvest, one of the fertility runes, and stands for the natural progression of life that must be followed and the effort that must be made to reap rewards. This is another rune for fertility and abundance in candle spells and also for a project that will not bear fruit for some time.

Lagu L is the lake or waters and is the rune of emotions and intuition. Use this rune on your candle for accepting change and for any matter of the heart or emotions (linked with Saille, the willow tree stave).

Man M is the rune of human life and mortality, and talks of realism and the need to fulfil one's own destiny. Engrave this rune to overcome loss and for forgiving weakness in self and others.

Ing makes the sound **Ng** on the end of a word. Ing was the old fertility god who died each autumn to be reborn the next year, and also the deity of protection of the household. Write this rune on your candle for spells for quiet sleep, for fertility and for protection.

Nyd N is another fire rune and talks of the old 'nyd' fires that were kindled by rubbing wood together and were used to light the festival fires (see Chapter 2). It represents needs that must be met from within us rather than looking to others. Use this rune for candle rituals concerning self-reliance and the ability to change as a person to meet new demands and life paths.

Odal O is the homestead that was very precious to wandering peoples. It is used to represent all domestic issues and is a protective rune of the home. Etch this on your candle for all matters concerning home, family and justice.

Peorth P is the rune cup that was used for gambling and divination; both were one and the same. The fall of the runes from the cup could express the will of the gods and the outcome of every venture. It therefore represents fate, in the sense that we all have a unique destiny to fulfil, and so is the essential self (see also Tinne, the holly in the tree staves). Use this symbol for core issues and ones where your identity is at stake.

Rad R is the wheel, whether the turning sun wheel, the wheel on the chariot of the old fertility god Ing or the wheel on wagons travelling to distant parts. It stands for change and action. Engrave this rune when you want any form of movement in your life, a new home, career, relationship or a change of scene.

Sigil S and **Z** is the rune of the sun and represents energy, light and limitless possibility. This will bring the uncovering of talents and fulfilment of dreams within the scope of your candle spell.

Tyr T is the star, the spirit warrior and god of war who sacrificed his sword arm to save the other gods. His letter therefore presents sacrifice for a long-term goal and altruism. This is the rune for kicking bad habits or for taking the honest option.

Thorn, which makes the sound **Th** or **The**, is both a protective and strength rune, being the mighty hammer of the god of thunder, Thor, and so represents might in the defence of others. This is a rune that in candle spells will protect you and those you love.

Ur U was the aurochs, the mighty horned cattle that roamed the plains of northern Europe until early in the seventeenth century. This rune letter therefore represents primal strength and survival. Etch this rune on your candle for a ritual that is a survival issue, or one where you need a great impetus to push through any change you desire.

Wyn V and **W** is the rune of pure joy and happiness, not through others but through the achievement of one's own dreams and unique life path (see also Muinn, the tree stave of joy). Use this rune in candle spells for personal happiness and for following your unique life path.

Eohl X is the eel grass that was harsh to touch but provided roofing, bedding and food for animals and so was of use once the initial pain was over (see also Onn, the tree stave of transformation). It has come to represent the need to grasp the nettle and show courage in a crisis, which will then lead to better things. Engrave this rune on a candle when you are seeking a new beginning after difficulty or need to accept the truth of a situation.

Yr or **Eoh Y** is the yew tree, the tree of endings, and therefore represents the need to move on to the next stage in life or a relationship (see also Ido, the yew in the tree staves).

The tree alphabet or Ogham staves

The tree alphabet, the magical alphabet of the Druids – the priests/bards of the Celts – has survived largely orally. For this reason, there are many disagreements about the definitive form of the symbols and even over which trees are included. The version I use below is one that has consistent features with several forms. The capitals were carved upright, the way I have used them for the staves, but were signed or etched horizontally for lower case letters and were sometimes joined. The staves were named after Ogma, Celtic warrior god, deity of wisdom and champion of the gods at the Battle of Moytura.

But the Ogham staves are not just alternative runes. They originate from a different culture – one of hills, bubbling streams and green groves. While the runes came from the world of winter, ice and snow, the tree staves are born of the spring, of hope and rising sap, of new life and optimism. This difference can be reflected in your choice of symbols for engraving, according to whether you need the sheer power of the Vikings or the gentler, more poetic energies of the Celts.

As with the runes, you can use a single stave instead of your name or wish if it contains the power that you are seeking: for example ┤ or Huathe, the hawthorn, can be engraved on your candle if you need courage. As with the runes, if you find a letter missing when using the Ogham script to write your name or wish, choose one similar in sound or omit it. It is the act of writing your name on the candle, not the spelling, that holds the magic.

Beith	Birch	B			Muinn	Vine/bramble	M	
Luis	Rowan	L			Gort	Ivy	G	
Fearn	Alder	F			Ngetal	Broom/fern	Ng	
Saille	Willow	S			Straif	Blackthorn	Str	
Nuinn	Ash	N			Ruis	Elder	R	
Huathe	Hawthorn/ whitethorn	H			Ailm	Fir/pine	A	
Duir	Oak	D			Onn	Furze/gorse	O	
Tinne	Holly	T			Ur	Heather	U	
Coll	Hazel	C			Edhadh	White poplar/ aspen	E	
Quert	Apple	Q			Ido	Yew	I	

Beith B, which means shining, indicates birth, new beginnings, opportunities and the purging of what is redundant or destructive. It is the stave of the innovator and can be used on your candle when carrying out a ritual for a fresh start or a fresh approach to an old problem.

Luis L, the rowan, sacred to the moon, is the stave of protection (especially for family matters) and can be engraved on candles for rituals concerning delicate negotiations, gaining the support of others and for the ability to overcome any difficulties, turning obstacles to advantage.

Fearn F, the alder tree, is a stave of fire, offering firm foundations and security, whether material, practical or emotional. It is the stave of practical matters and money and so can be engraved to ensure the fruition of realistic plans.

Saille S, the willow, another moon stave, is for rebirth and regeneration, especially the regeneration of inspiration after a stagnant period, as well as intuition and all emotional matters. This stave can bring intuitive wisdom and aid love rituals.

Nuinn N, the ash, is a tree of expansion of possibility and of confidence, and is associated with travel and with astral projection; this symbol will therefore focus energies for positive change and learning.

Huathe H, the hawthorn or whitethorn, represents resilience and courage and a shield against psychic as well as physical harm. It is therefore a good symbol to engrave on candles when you feel under any kind of threat, and represents the power to fight for what is right and the determination to achieve objectives, no matter what the cost.

Duir D, the oak tree, is the Druidic symbol of endurance, power, strength and assertiveness, tempered with nobility, idealism and altruism. Engrave this on your candle as a stave of power for any ambition.

Tinne T, the holly, stands for fate, placing any advantage or reversal as part of a long-term plan, so that each stage that should be enjoyed or endured and used as a building block for a long-term future plan. Add this to your candle if you feel a victim of fate and are struggling to control your destiny.

Coll C, the hazel, is the Celtic tree of wisdom, traditional knowledge and justice. The stave invites a measured response to life and decisions based on all the facts rather than emotion. Etched on a candle, it can be helpful for spells about justice or decision-making, and also for divination.

Quert Q, the apple, is the Celtic tree of life, youth, health, fertility and abundance. Apple bobbing is an old form of Druidic love divination, to discover who of a group of young maidens would first be married. In the modern world, fertility is not only of the soil and of people but extends to any aspect of life that needs renewing, especially health. Engrave your candle with this stave for fertility, health and spells for increasing inner radiance.

Muinn M, the vine or bramble, is the tree stave of pure joy, enthusiasm and the confidence that all will be well. Carve it for spells for self-love and esteem, and for happiness.

Gort G, the ivy, is the stave of relationships and loyalty. The ivy came to be associated primarily with fidelity and was worn in bridal headdresses long before the adoption of orange blossom. Its symbolism can be extended to all stable relationships, and so this symbol is powerful in candle rituals for family matters, marriage and friendship, and for the renewal of trust.

Ngetal Ng, the broom or fern, is the stave of prosperity. Because it blooms golden at midsummer, the association with the height of the sun's power made it a symbol of gold and riches. Ngetal is therefore a good focus not only for money spells and business endeavours, but also for uncovering hidden talents.

Straif Str, the blackthorn, is the stave of effort and persistence. Because it blooms when the bitter north-east winds are at their height, a harsh winter is called a blackthorn winter. Etch Straif for concentrated energy, supreme will and persistence in the face of any challenge, as well as for unity with others.

Ruis R, the elder tree, is the stave of second sight and also for the unexpected. The elder is the ultimate fairy tree; it is said that if you wear a crown of elder twigs on May Eve (30 April) you will be able to see magical creatures and ghosts. Native Americans call the elder the 'tree of music'. Inscribe Ruis on your candle for divinatory purposes and also for inspiration if there seems no answer to a problem.

Ailm A, the fir or pine, is the stave of clarity, communication and creation. Ailm represents the inner creation moving into the outer world, the new idea being put into practice, just as the pine torch casts its fire to illuminate the darkness within the ancient halls. Engrave it when you need to increase your influence and to persuade others.

Onn O, the furze or gorse, is the stave of transformation and positive change. Just as spring transforms the dead world of winter and burning transforms the gorse into food for animals as new, softer shoots push through the ground, so the energies of the Onn stave stand for change whereby one stage of life is transformed into another by 'grasping the nettle'. Use this stave in your candle magic if you fear change and for the power to adapt to new, challenging situations.

Ur U, the heather, represents both strong emotions and passionate feelings, as well as eternal love: in Celtic legend, when Oscar, son of Ossian the renowned Irish bard and warrior-hero of the third century, lay dying on the battlefield at Ulster, he sent his true love Malvina a sprig of purple heather. Use this stave in spells not only for passionate love, but also for any ritual where you seek to follow or speak what is in your heart.

Edhadh E, the white poplar or aspen tree, is the stave of healing. Because the white poplar is associated with the last harvest and the autumn of life, it is a stave that stands for fruition – whether of a project or a relationship – and also for reconciling whatever is unfair or lost and cannot be regained. Use the stave on your candle for healing spells, for reconciliation and for happiness based on experience.

Ido I, the yew, is the stave of immortality and rebirth. Associated with the turning of the wheel of existence and the death aspect of the triple goddess, Ido is the stave of endings, transformation and rebirth. As an old trunk decays it is replaced by a new one inside, and so in candle rituals it can herald a new beginning after closing doors.

Birth **sun signs**

You can carve your own astrological sun sign on a candle to represent yourself, or that of another person for whom the candle stands. You can also strengthen any ritual by etching the symbol of the current sun sign period on the opposite side of the candle from your name or wish. Carving a specific sun sign is also a way of adding to your candle ritual any of the strengths associated with that sign.

Aries, the Ram (21 March–20 April): A fire sign, for all matters of the self and of identity, and for all rituals of innovation, assertiveness and action.

Taurus, the Bull (21 April–21 May): An earth sign, for rituals concerning material matters and security; also for patience and caution if the way ahead seems hazardous.

Gemini, the Heavenly Twins (22 May–21 June): An air sign, for spells concerning adaptability, communication, learning, choices to be made and short-distance travel.

Cancer, the Crab (22 June–22 July): A water sign, for spells concerning the home and family, especially for protection and for gentle love and friendship.

Leo, the Lion (23 July–23 August): A fire sign, for rituals for courage and leadership, for all sensual pleasures, and love affairs.

Virgo, the Maiden (24 August–22 September): An earth sign, for spells to increase efficiency, for bringing order to a chaotic and troubled situation, for self-improvement and for healing.

Libra, the Scales (23 September–23 October): An air sign, for rituals concerning justice and the law, for balancing options and priorities, and for relationships, harmony and reconciliation.

Scorpio, the Scorpion (24 October–22 November): A water sign for increasing second sight, for passion and sex, for secrets, for inheritance and for claiming what is rightfully yours in any area of life.

Sagittarius, the Archer (23 November–21 December): A fire sign for optimism, for clarity of vision and focus, for long-distance travel and house moves, and for expanding horizons.

Capricorn, the Goat (22 December–20 January): An earth sign, for ambitions, perseverance, matters concerning officialdom, loyalty and for the acquisition of money.

Aquarius, the Water Carrier (21 January–18 February): An air sign, for independence, friendship, creativity and detachment from emotional blackmail.

Pisces, the Fish (19 February–20 March): A water sign, for spells to develop spiritual awareness and intuition, for divination (especially involving water) and the fulfilment of hidden dreams.

Christine's **candle wishes**

Christine is a single parent who had fallen in love with Tom, a kind, gentle man ten years her junior who had admitted that he had been in trouble with the law several times for petty crimes, but was now determined to go straight. She had her own home, but Tom had asked her to sell up and move north with him so that they could start afresh, as they both lived in a small village where they were the subject of gossip.

- Christine decided to light a yellow candle for travel and moving house, but wrote her wish on white paper for a new beginning for herself, Tom and her young daughter, who is devoted to Tom and whose own father has emigrated. She used ordinary writing as her wish was long and complex, and as she wrote she felt that her own position was becoming clearer:

  I wish to sell my house quickly for a good price so that we can start afresh. I also wish that Tom and I will find good jobs in the north so that finances will be less of a struggle.

- On the front of the paper she entwined the birth signs of herself and Tom: ♉ Taurus, her own sign, which also stabilizes the spell with its inbuilt patience, and ♐ Sagittarius, Tom's sign, which also represents house moves and long-distance travel, as well as his natural optimism. Because the wish was so crucial, Christine engraved ⊦ Beith, the birch tree stave for new beginnings, on one side of her candle, entwined with ᛒ Beorc, the birch tree of the runes that is also associated with rebirth and new life.

- Christine carried out the ritual on a Sunday and so engraved the sun ☉ on the other side of the candle, another powerful symbol of regeneration and energy.

- Finally, she dressed the candle with an oil fragranced with mint for money, travel and house moves, repeating as she worked:

  Bring me a new happy home.

- Christine lit the candle and sat looking into the flame, visualizing a new life with Tom and her daughter. She placed the wish taper in the flame. Initially, it appeared to go out, but it remained alight, burning slowly but steadily, suggesting that there might be initial difficulties, but that with perseverance she would succeed.

- Christine collected the ash from the paper and placed it on dark paper, shaking it to make a picture. She saw a figure going away from a house towards mountains and interpreted that Tom was going first to find a job, an option she had not considered.

- She then dripped wax from the yellow wish candle on to the ash, and the picture changed to show a high fence between the house and hills. What was the fence? *'My own doubts'*, Christine said spontaneously, and for the first time examined her own fears about uprooting with her daughter for an uncertain future; these were not an insurmountable barrier but had to be faced now rather than when it was too late. She left the candle to burn and the wax formed a long road.

- Christine decided that Tom should go first to find a job, and then if they felt the same by the time the house was sold, she could follow him. Alternatively, she had the option of buying a new property in the nearest town, where she had grown up and which she missed greatly.

A wish may change after we have made it, but this is a good focus to discover what we truly want.

CHAPTER SEVEN

Protective Candles

We all feel vulnerable at some time in our lives and though, unlike our forebears, we may not face wild beasts or hostile tribes, the dangers of the modern world may be no less daunting. We may fear for any members of our family who are out at night or far away, especially if they are young. In the night, fears and worries can be magnified, causing nightmares or insomnia, and if you are sensitive – as most people who develop their intuitive powers through magic or divination are – you will be more vulnerable than many others to petty spite and gossip.

Hostility from the outside world may not always be deliberate, nor does it necessarily come from someone who has cause to hate us: a sarcastic shop assistant, a rude bus driver, a difficult colleague or boss may all vent their own bad feelings on us in passing – but the draining effects are the same. Add together the tensions of family members or flatmates arriving home tired and hungry, and you may feel as though an exorcism is needed to dissipate the snarling demons that lurk at the door.

Our ancestors burned fires to keep away dangers, both earthly and less tangible. Equally, candles can melt away negative feelings that enter the home from the outside world, replacing them with harmony and positiveness.

Protective **fragrances**

The simplest way of restoring harmony to your home is to burn candles or oils in burners using protective fragrances. You can buy scented candles in tins that you can place in the entrance hall, around the main living area and in the bedrooms. The best oil burners have a dish shape on top for the oils, to which you can add a few drops of water, and a place for a night light or a very small candle underneath.

Use more vigorous scents to cleanse away initial or lingering negativity, then as the evening progresses and in areas where you relax, you can burn the softer fragrances as moods correspondingly mellow.

Powerful cleansers of negativity include bay, cedarwood, cypress, frankincense, juniper, peppermint, pine, rosemary, sage and thyme. Burn these fragrances near entrances to purify outside influences and to deflect any lingering or incipient family quarrels. If you have an open fire, you can also place two or three drops of cedar, pine or rosemary oil directly on to the logs. Oil burners or fragrant candles are also good in dining areas, where discussions may tip over into arguments or, if you have a family, food fads may cause unresolved anger to flare.

Gentle, restorative fragrances include geranium, lavender, rosewood, rose, sandalwood and ylang ylang. Burn these in areas where you relax, to soothe hyperactive children and teenagers, and to slow down workaholic adults. Rose and lavender perfumed night lights are especially potent when burned in a child's bedroom before he or she goes to bed, and the scent will linger.

If you have a difficult or critical family member, friend or neighbour coming to visit, light your gentle fragrances before they arrive. Your guest will be visibly less strident, and you also will be more relaxed and less sensitive to barbs unwitting or intended.

Creating sentinels *of light*

In Chapter 15, I describe how candles symbolizing the archangels at the four main compass points can offer protection. I have found this especially effective for protecting your home if you need to leave it empty for a few days. This concept goes back to the ancient idea of earth 'dwights' or guardians, who stood sentinel over areas of land and villages, protecting them at night. If you do not find the concept of angels one to which you can relate, envisage your protective guardians as pillars of light, with or without features.

- Position four tall white candles at the four main compass points around the room. In summer you could use outdoor candles, perhaps in a protective fragrance such as citronella (which is also excellent for repelling insects) to surround your home if it is detached, or in the outermost corners of your front and back gardens.
- As dusk falls, or at any time when you need to leave your home unattended for a long period, begin first with the candle of the north. Say as you light it:

Candle of the north, release the guardian of the rocks, the stones and the living crystals to stand watch over my home and

those within, that it may be impenetrable as a fortress against any who would enter and do harm.

Visualize light radiating from the flame and forming a brilliant laser beam eastwards in an arc extending to the candle of the east.

- Light next the candle of the east, saying:

Candle of the east, release the guardian of the rushing winds, wild mountaintops and boundless skies, to stand watch over my home and those therein, repelling with your mighty blasts all who would intrude with bad intent.

Visualize its beams forming an arc of light to the candle of the south.

- Light the candle of the south, saying:

Candle of the south, release the guardian of the blazing sun, the lightning flash and volcanoes to stand watch on my home and sear with your heat all who would invade my sanctuary from the world.

Visualize its light rays extending to the candle of the west.

- Finally, light the candle of the west, saying:

Candle of the west, release the guardian of the boiling sea, the rushing torrents and the cascading waterfalls to stand watch over my home and its occupants and form a moat of protection too deep and wide for any to cross with malice.

Visualize its light moving northwards, to form an unbroken circle of light which expands until it encloses the whole house, above and around as far as your boundaries, the front and back gates or walls, or the extent of your lobby space in an apartment. Make a gesture as you stand bathed in light, for example drawing a circle on your palm and saying:

When I make this sign, my inner candles will instantly erect my protective barrier of light around my home and its occupants.

- Blow out the candles, beginning in the west and proceeding anti-clockwise. Watch the circle of light fade, but not disappear. The candle guardians can be activated whenever you need them, but you should renew the protective circle regularly by lighting the candles and recreating the circle. Once a month, on or close to the night of the full moon, light the four candles and leave them to burn right out, repeating the words you have spoken in your mind.

Personal **protection**

Your sentinels of light will protect your home and its occupants while you relax and sleep, but there are many occasions when we are at work or away from home when we can sense the negativity or even emotional demands of others sapping our energy and undermining our self-confidence. If you know that you are going to be in a difficult or potentially confrontational situation, or are going to meet people who depress or drain you psychologically, create a personal light shield that, like your home guardians, can be erected instantly when negative influences threaten your harmony.

Drawing a circle of light *from a candle ring*

This ritual is best practised at noon, so that the candle power is amplified by the sun at its height. If you can work indoors in the centre of a pool of light, with the candles framed in shadow, you can draw maximum energy. You can also experiment with different angled lamps to create the supplementary pool of light, if the sun is not in the right place for your ritual.

If it is a dull day, use more or brighter candles to compensate for the lack of light. I am writing this as the shortest day of the year approaches and though it is midday, the light has barely broken through. Surround yourself with a ring of small golden candles, if possible round ones, the shape of the sun. Buy a store of these for the rest of the year at Christmas, when they are cheap and plentiful. Candlelight can give you extra energy on a dull day.

○ Begin in the south, the direction of the noonday sun, and light your candles in turn clockwise, saying:

Burn bright, candlelight,
Drive away all danger,
Protect me as I work and live,
From false friend and stranger.

Repeat this over and over until you are surrounded by a complete circle of light. Now turn nine times clockwise within the circle of candles and sunshine, repeating the invocation. The sun will make the candle seem brighter.

○ Sit within the circle of light and see it hardening like a transparent, golden crystal shield above your head, below your feet and all around in a sphere. Extend your hands so that you can feel its edges.

○ You now need to decide on your activation mechanism for times when you cannot light a candle ring, perhaps touching your unseen psychic 'third eye' on your brow, in the position between and just above your physical eyes. As you do so, say:

When I awaken my third eye by touching it, I will automatically bring to life my candle circle of safety.

○ Blow out your candles anti-clockwise, beginning with the one immediately to the right of your southernmost candle, so that the last candle alight is the first one you ignited. See the light fade, but know that it is always there to be activated in times of need. Repeat your candle ritual regularly whenever needed.

Protecting **children**

I have already mentioned that lavender and rose candles are good for soothing insomnia and hyperactivity in children. Young children who suffer from nightmares or fear of the dark, or who may be going through a difficult period – perhaps of teasing or bullying at school – may find a bedtime candle ritual soothing. Used with care, candles can give children immense comfort.

A bedtime **ritual**

You do not have to use a perfumed candle. Any gentle shade of pink or purple is good for healing emotional wounds.

- Let the child take a bath to which two or three drops of chamomile, rose or lavender have been added. If your child has skin allergies, these oils usually help – but do check with a physician first.
- In the meantime, place a large pastel candle on a safe surface in the bedroom, but do not light it. Take 12 rose quartz or amethyst crystals, or glass nuggets in pink and lilac. Jade is another gentle stone that is suitable for protecting children.
- When your child is ready for bed, ask him or her to make a crystal castle in the shape of a square around the candle, beginning in the direction that is approximately north. The square is the shape of limitation within time and space, and so is very good for earthing a little one whose nocturnal imagination is running riot. It is also an excellent geometric form for security rituals.
- Before the child is in bed, light the candle and, holding your child's power hand (the one he or she draws with) in yours, trace the towers of the castle, the door and drawbridge enclosing the protective flame. Pull up the invisible drawbridge and together blow out the candle, visualizing the light rising upwards and creating a larger castle around the child's bed. Say together:

None may come within my candlelight castle until the sun breaks through.

- Remove the candle from the room, so that the little one is not tempted to try to relight it, but leave the crystals in place if your child is old enough not to put them in his or her mouth. A large, unpolished chunk of rose quartz or amethyst can be substituted to hold the crystal candlelight for very small children. Open the curtains so that the child can see the star 'candles' in the sky, and leave on a pink-shaded lamp if the infant is still nervous.
- Repeat the ritual nightly for a week and at times of stress.

Protection **on a journey**

However careful we may be, we can find ourselves in a situation where we have to cross a deserted car park, or wait on a station platform or taxi rank late at night, and the more anxious we feel, the more attention it seems we attract. Many of the old defensive spells offered invisibility – not in a literal sense, but by lowering our visibility threshold to others by casting a greyness so that we merge with the surroundings.

Making a magical wax protection amulet

A traditional way of invoking this protection is to make a wax amulet, carved with a magical square of protection. Although it is very fragile, you can make one for a special journey and renew it when it becomes cracked. This is a good way of keeping the energies topped up.

- Use a wide, short, dark grey or brown candle for invisibility or a deep green one to enfold yourself in love. Light it at dusk, if possible on a misty day.
- Place the candle directly in a fireproof tray rather than in a holder and let the candle wax melt away, spreading it so that it forms a square. When the wax is set, ease it from the tray with a wooden spatula or (very gently) with a knife.
- You can now carve a protective word square with an awl, nail or large pin on the wax tablet, perhaps with your astrological sun sign on the back. Word squares were created by writing what were usually corruptions of medieval Latin

words forwards, backwards, up and down. The words used sound strange when translated and were probably originally brought into popular usage by servants of high magicians or even via lay brothers in monasteries. Although illiterate or semi-literate, they may have seen certain words used in spells or religious ceremonies of exorcism, and then copied them out of the original context.

The magic comes from the repeated association of the same word over centuries with protection, love, banishing or wealth, rather like a psychic snowball. When it is written or engraved, and endowed with the hopes of the creator, the power or protection is activated.

One of the most common protective word squares was written on either parchment or wax and worn around the neck in a red cotton bag, a colour and fabric associated with the Norse mother goddess Frigg. You can etch this on your wax:

```
S A T O R
A R E P O
T E N E T
O P E R A
R O T A S
```

○ In accordance with tradition, make all the letters the same size, work from left to right, top to bottom, and do not let your shadow fall on what you have etched as you work. Sator means literally 'the sower'. Arepo is a plough, Tenet means 'he, she or it holds'. Opera are works or tasks, and Rotas wheels in the accusative or object case. None of the words are magical in themselves, but – like all magical objects – are endowed with significance by the emotions with which they are entwined.

○ When your amulet is finished, wrap it gently in gauze or cottonwool and keep it in a small red bag of any fabric for protection when you travel.

CHAPTER EIGHT

Candle Rituals

Once you know the colour and fragrance correspondences given in Chapters 4 and 5, you can devise your own candle rituals. Here is some basic background information about magical practices, including the traditional timings.

Candles and **the moon**

Candle ceremonies fall mainly under the auspices of the moon, whose different phases offer us specific energies. If you are not an experienced moon watcher, most daily newspapers will give you the daily moon phase in their weather section.

Although the moon is often regarded as having three phases – waxing, full and waning, which correspond in ancient religions with the maiden, mother and crone triple goddess – the number of days that fall into each cycle vary with the month. It may therefore be easier to divide the moon's cycle into two periods, each of approximately 14 days.

The waxing moon

The moon is in its waxing cycle as it moves from the new moon to the full moon. As the moon grows or increases, so it can give power to all rituals for growth and increase – whether in health, love, knowledge or prosperity. The waxing moon is the traditional 'planting' period, whether for herbs and vegetables or for conceiving a baby. Use white or pale-coloured candles for your waxing moon rituals, with silver on the day of the full moon.

The day of the full moon is very effective for all spells for power, ambition and success, for the climax of endeavours and for sex magic. Full moon energies span from three days before to three days after the full moon day.

The waning moon

The moon wanes as it moves from full moon to new moon again. As the visible moon decreases in size, it is reflected in weakening power in human endeavour. The traditional time for harvesting herbs and flowers or pruning trees, this period is therefore potent for removing negative influences, shedding redundant guilt or resentment, ending destructive relationships, reducing pain (especially chronic), and for giving up addictions and compulsions. The waning moon is also good for scrying.

The dark of the moon – the three days when the old moon is invisible and the crescent not yet discernible to the human eye – is said to be best for rituals of protection and for any undertaking that involves secrecy. Use darker candles: purple or blue for this cycle, with brown or black for the dark of the moon.

Solar times **for candle rituals**

Where lunar time suggests the best times of the month for specific rituals, solar times refine these to times of the day when the energies are in tune with different aspects of life.

Dawn is good for magic regarding new beginnings, change and gain, whether in love, money, health or happiness.

Noon is for action, power and success. It may sound strange to perform candle rituals in the middle of the day, but sunbeams dancing around a flame, especially if you have crystals or mirrors to reflect the rainbows, combine the power of the flame with the fire of the sun. If you need a surge of power or have an urgent need, candle magic at noon on the days of the full moon provides a focus that concentrates the greatest solar and lunar powers.

Dusk is for love, healing and banishing any guilt, resentment or regrets accumulated during the day. In the Jewish religion, candles lit just before dusk on a Friday herald the Sabbath and so candle magic at dusk is especially significant for family matters.

Midnight candle rituals bring acceptance and balance, when there is no conscious thought, anxiety or even forward planning, but an opening to the darkness within and beyond. If you cannot sleep, light a purple candle scented with lavender and let the midnight energies, whether moonlit or dark, wipe the slate clean, so that you sleep until dawn.

Days of the week *and their planetary associations*

Each day of the week is associated with one of the original seven planets visible to the naked eye. Since each planet became associated with the qualities of the classical deity whose name it bears, each day focuses on a specific area of need. These planetary associations also apply to the magical hours that are listed on page 69.

The sun
Sunday, the day of the sun, is for candle spells if the main focus is on a personal need, concerned with your identity and individuality; it is potent also for energy, joy, prosperity, spiritual awareness, self-knowledge, luck, power, promotion, good fortune, success and ambition.

The moon
Monday, the day of the moon, is for all candle rites concerning partnership issues or the need to make a choice, especially where there are no clear pointers ahead; it is also for protection, psychic development, clairvoyance and meaningful dreams, emotions, the sea, home, gardening, female fertility, animals and children. Moon magic restores the natural cycles and energy flows.

Mars

Tuesday, the day of Mars, is for candle spells if you are concerned with expansion in any field, face opposition, need courage, feel strongly about an issue or seek change; it is for action of all kinds, and for passion and male sexuality.

Mercury

Wednesday, the day of Mercury, is for candle rituals for travel, communication of any kind, health, mental clarity, business negotiations, money and overcoming debts.

Jupiter

Thursday, the day of Jupiter, is for candle divination and astral projection, or for spells for career matters, examinations, learning, male fertility, expansion, giving, altruism and ideals, justice and the law.

Venus

Friday, the day of Venus, is for matters concerning peace, romance, love, relationships, family and friendship, pleasure, art, music, physical beauty, and female health and sexuality.

Saturn

Saturday, the day of Saturn, is concerned with unfinished business, endings that lead to beginnings, and the unexpected. So it is a good day for candle rituals for all slow-moving matters and for accepting limitations, as well as for overcoming obstacles, lifting depression or doubts, for meditation and psychic defence, and for locating lost objects, animals and people.

The planetary hours

In this system, the magical periods are not exact hours from 6am sunrise to 6pm sunset, but are calculated from the actual (varying) daily sunrise to the actual (varying) sunset – both of which you can find in a diary or newspaper.

- The actual day length is divided by 12 to give you the daytime periods. This means that in summer each period will be longer than an hour and in winter shorter. The only exception is at the equinoxes, when day and night are equal.
- The sunset to sunrise length divided by 12 will give you the night-time periods; again, these will not be exactly 60 minutes but will vary according to the time of year.
- Each of these periods, day and night, is ruled by a different planet according to the day of the week on which it falls.

If, for example, you were carrying out a ritual for a new beginning in your career, you would begin on the new moon at dawn, the first hour – Jupiter's hour – on Thursday, the day of Jupiter who governs career. If the spell was to be carried out for three days, you would choose Jupiter's hour on Friday (the fifth hour) and on Saturday (the second hour).

Many practitioners save the planetary hours for important or complex spells.

Candles with several wicks can be lit over a period of days for continuing rituals.

Daytime: sunrise to sunset

Add the hours and minutes from sunrise to sunset and divide the total by 12 to give you the periods for each day. If you wish, you can calculate a week or month ahead, using the table below as a basis. Remember to allow for local and regional variations.

The first 'hour' period each day at sunrise is ruled by its day planet. As you will see, the planetary order has a regular pattern.

Hour	Sunday	Monday	Tuesday	Wednesday	Thursday	Friday	Saturday
1	Sun	Moon	Mars	Mercury	Jupiter	Venus	Saturn
2	Venus	Saturn	Sun	Moon	Mars	Mercury	Jupiter
3	Mercury	Jupiter	Venus	Saturn	Sun	Moon	Mars
4	Moon	Mars	Mercury	Jupiter	Venus	Saturn	Sun
5	Saturn	Sun	Moon	Mars	Mercury	Jupiter	Venus
6	Jupiter	Venus	Saturn	Sun	Moon	Mars	Mercury
7	Mars	Mercury	Jupiter	Venus	Saturn	Sun	Moon
8	Sun	Moon	Mars	Mercury	Jupiter	Venus	Saturn
9	Venus	Saturn	Sun	Moon	Mars	Mercury	Jupiter
10	Mercury	Jupiter	Venus	Saturn	Sun	Moon	Mars
11	Moon	Mars	Mercury	Jupiter	Venus	Saturn	Sun
12	Saturn	Sun	Moon	Mars	Mercury	Jupiter	Venus

Night-time: sunset to sunrise

Hour	Sunday	Monday	Tuesday	Wednesday	Thursday	Friday	Saturday
1	Jupiter	Venus	Saturn	Sun	Moon	Mars	Mercury
2	Mars	Mercury	Jupiter	Venus	Saturn	Sun	Moon
3	Sun	Moon	Mars	Mercury	Jupiter	Venus	Saturn
4	Venus	Saturn	Sun	Moon	Mars	Mercury	Jupiter
5	Mercury	Jupiter	Venus	Saturn	Sun	Moon	Mars
6	Moon	Mars	Mercury	Jupiter	Venus	Saturn	Sun
7	Saturn	Sun	Moon	Mars	Mercury	Jupiter	Venus
8	Jupiter	Venus	Saturn	Sun	Moon	Mars	Mercury
9	Mars	Mercury	Jupiter	Venus	Saturn	Sun	Moon
10	Sun	Moon	Mars	Mercury	Jupiter	Venus	Saturn
11	Venus	Saturn	Sun	Moon	Mars	Mercury	Jupiter
12	Mercury	Jupiter	Venus	Saturn	Sun	Moon	Mars

Joanne's **two-day candle ritual**

A run of bad luck can make us feel as though we are on a downward spiral from which we cannot escape. Bad things do happen out of the blue to most people at some time, but when we become (quite naturally) depressed and disillusioned, our co-ordination gets worse, making us accident prone. It is easy to lose possessions, because our memory is affected by worry. Joanne needed to halt the cycle and restore optimism, so that she could respond more positively to life and thereby attract good vibrations.

She decided that Saturday, the day of Saturn, would be a good day for the first part of this ritual, after dusk at the hour of Saturn. She would then begin a new luck cycle on the Sunday, the day of new beginnings, at dawn on the sun's own hour.

Ideally, Joanne would have carried out the first part of the ritual on the last day of the old moon for any banishing energies, but rarely do our needs fall so neatly into place. Since it was a waxing moon cycle, she carefully scratched the waning moon sign on her banishing candle.

Day 1: Ending the bad luck

○ Joanne used a tall black candle to represent the run of bad luck that had included having her car stolen, losing her job and finding out that her best friend had been seeing her boyfriend behind her back. (Some practitioners use an additional grey candle alongside the black, which they move closer to absorb the bad luck from the black candle.) She encircled the black candle with five orange candles for the sun and new life.

○ At dusk on Saturday she lit the black candle, saying:

Let my bad luck burn away.

○ She then took a length of wool, knotted it, and burned it in the flame, saying:

Ill fortune be gone.

Joanne named each of her pieces of ill fortune in a separate knotted thread and burned it, repeating each time:

Ill fortune, be gone.

○ When all were burned, she took a white taper and from the black candle lit the first orange candle directly to the north, the realm of midnight, saying:

From evil comes good, from sorrow, joy, bad luck change so to good fortune.

At this point she extinguished the black candle, saying:

Burn no more. Your power is done.

○ Joanne then lit the second orange candle from the first using a taper, saying:

Fortune grow and flame.

She then continued around the circle until all five orange candles were alight.

○ In the growing darkness, Joanne sat watching the circle of candles and let them burn out, except for the last – in the west of the circle, the position of the setting sun. This she blew out almost as soon as it was kindled, saying:

Carry the flame of good fortune till tomorrow.

Day 2: Bringing good fortune

○ Joanne placed her final unburned orange candle in the centre of the circle and lit it at dawn on Sunday (the hour of the sun), saying:

Good luck rekindle and increase.

○ Surrounding the orange candle, she had placed five tall, golden sun candles. These she lit with a white taper from the orange candle, beginning with the one in the east for the new day. As she lit each in turn from the previous one, using a taper, she said:

Good luck grow, fortune smile on me and let the joy increase.

○ Joanne let all the candles except the one in the south burn down. This she kept for any time that her confidence wavered or met a setback. When she did waver, she set up a new good luck cycle with the unburned sun candle surrounded by new orange candles. Again, she kept the last unburned candle for future rituals, this time using the single orange candle surrounded by gold ones. In this way, the candle good luck cycle can be continued to strengthen our will in meeting the problems that life throws at us.

Seasonal Candle Magic

Living in towns and cities, it is very easy to miss the passing of the seasons. With artificial lighting, central heating and the availability of once seasonal foods from around the world, all year round, we have lost touch with our own rhythms and the natural fluctuations of our spiritual as well as bodily energies. These inner tides mirror the natural seasons: for example, slowing down in winter when working hours were limited by daylight, and the long days of summer that created an upsurge of energy to gather in the crops, are cycles that trace back through our genetic inheritance to our ancestral lands. So, if you hail from northern climes but live in Florida, Durban or Sydney, you may still feel a seemingly irrational desire to hibernate in late November.

The recently recognized Seasonal Affective Disorder (SAD), which seems to cause depression and inertia through lack of sunlight, may occur because we need to operate at full peak when our body clock is telling us to rest in our cave.

The eightfold *division of the year*

The northern tradition divides the calendar into four seasons: spring, summer, autumn and winter. However, this can vary in other parts of the world. The ancient Egyptians, for example, recognized only three seasons: *akhet,* the season of sowing, *pert,* the season of growing, and *semut,* the season of harvest. In magic, the eightfold division of the year cuts across any differences and is the system used here.

Once the hunter-gatherer tribes had been superseded by the farmers of the neolithic period, the ritual year became inextricably linked with sowing and reaping, with the slaughter or bringing in of animals from the fields for winter, and the need to cleanse them when the summer began and they were set free to breed. These celebrations became endowed with the hopes, fears, love, hate and dreams of many generations. By the time the Celts enshrined the eightfold division of the year as a spiritual as well as a practical division of time, it was etched in the consciousness of the northern peoples. Even today, the call of the seasons can be felt in the highest office or apartment block in the middle of a city of millions.

Modern Wiccans, who follow a religion based on valuing nature, use candles as an important part of their eight major festivals, which are based on the old Celtic wheel of the year. If you live in the southern hemisphere, you can either follow the northern tradition or move your celebrations around six months, so that your spring equinox falls in mid-September, and so on.

Each season has its own candle colours and fragrances that can be incorporated not only into the celebrations of the festival days, but throughout the period

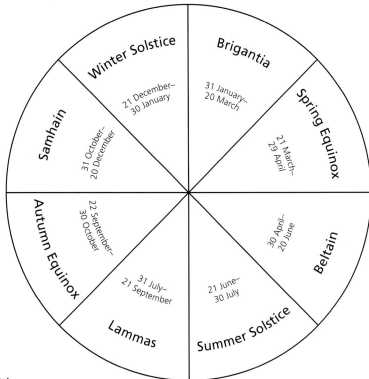

The wheel of the year.

ruled by the festival. The Celtic day began at sunset and so it is often the evening of these festivals – for example, Hallowe'en – that has retained its significance, as the true beginning of the new period.

You can enter the wheel of the year at any point. The Celtic year began at Samhain or Hallowe'en on 31 October and so this can strictly be regarded as the beginning. The wheel is constantly turning, and for many of us the true entry point falls during the period in which we are born.

I have started my wheel with Brigantia, the first festival to follow the relatively modern New Year transition on 1 January (adopted in Britain in 1752). It can be located on the wheel in the north-east compass position.

The festival dates that coincide with the solstices and equinoxes vary slightly from year to year, so check them on your calendar.

Seasonal rituals are not usually for instant love, happiness or riches, but rely on gradual growth if they are attracting spells or gradual decline if banishing, within a six-week period, using the natural flows and ebbs to carry them along.

Brigantia (Imbolc, Olmelc)

The festival of early spring is celebrated from sunset on 31 January to sunset on 2 February and embraces the Christian festival of Candlemas. It is described briefly in Chapter 2.

Its energies last until the eve of the spring equinox. This is a time for rituals concerning the first flowering of love or friendship, the rebirth of trust after a

A Brigantia spell for **new love and trust**

If you do not carry out this ritual during the three-day Brigantia period, try to perform it on the crescent moon or during the early waxing phase. It can lighten any dark winter or early spring morning.

○ Make a circle of eight alternate small pink and white candles, positioned in the wheel of the year formation.

○ Find the north-east position, either by using a compass or by making an approximate assessment. Beginning here, light incense outside the candle circle, then in turn at the south-east, the south-west and the north-west positions. The incenses of Brigantia include basil, benzoin, cedar and myrrh.

○ Next take a dish of milk or cream and two sprigs of any budding tree or evergreen: myrtle or ivy are symbols of faithful love, or you can use two snowdrops, crocuses or violets – all Brigantia flowers

and symbols of budding love and trust. Light your candles, starting with the candle of the north-east, saying:

Winter is in decline. I hold the first shoots of hope in my hand.

○ Pick up in turn the two symbols of new growth and circle each nine times around your candle, saying for each:

Sun of early spring grow stronger, that you may melt the lingering ice and warm my heart.

○ Place the dish of milk or cream in the centre of the candle circle and light the second candle at the due east position, saying:

Sun of early spring increase the light, until equal day vies with night and overcomes the darkness.

○ Dip each of the greenery sprigs or early flowers into the milk or

cream in turn, rubbing three drops on each stem and saying:

Milk flow after the dearth of winter, feed my heart and soul that it may grow once more whole and ready for love.

○ Bind the two flowers or the greenery together with pink ribbon, knotted six times – the number of Venus and love. Place them in front of the dish of milk or cream within the candle circle, saying:

In trust, I move closer, in friendship I seek to bind myself to [name]. Heal, mend and grow together.

○ Now light the other candles in turn, seeing light and the sun coming back into your life. Let them burn out naturally and when they have, set your flowers or greenery in a vase of water. Replace them when they begin to wilt, until you can feel the spell beginning to take effect.

setback and optimism after the long winter. In earlier times, the first ewe's milk was available to the community, and at the beginning of February snowdrops are pushing through the frozen soil. It is no coincidence that St Valentine's Day is marked in the modern calendar on 14 February, which was also the day, according to the legend chronicled by Chaucer, on which birds chose a mate. The same day was also the Roman Lupercalia, which was primarily a festival of youth. Lupercus was the Roman version of the nature deity Pan, who himself evolved from the horned god of animals and the hunt.

The most potent candle spells for love, friendship and trust will be performed on the actual festival, but they are also effective during the six weeks of the Brigantia period. In addition, such spells can be used at any time of year using symbols of Brigantia when you need to focus on this area of your life.

First-flowering rituals are gentle and good if you have been hurt or lack confidence; by the second spring around Easter, you will be filled with new optimism and any new relationships should be developing slowly and steadily.

White, cream and pink or any pale shade are the colours associated with innocence and gentleness.

The **spring equinox**

This falls around 21 March, depending on the year, and marks the return of the sun after winter. The old festival runs from sunset on the equinox eve for three days, but its energies last until sunset on 30 May, the beginning of Beltain or Beltane, the coming of summer. It is the time of year when, in the old Celtic tradition, the god of light overcame the god of darkness and marked the coming of days that were longer than night.

The equinox is, then, a time of rebirth and resurrection of joy, energy and, above all, new beginnings, whether for a new career, a new stage in your life or a sudden determination to follow a particular path. The energies are more powerful than those of Brigantia since the sun's rays are more powerful, but it is still associated with growth over a period after an initial surge.

Easter is the Christian celebration most closely associated with the spring equinox (see the Easter Eve ritual in Chapter 2). Wake at dawn on equinox morn or Easter Sunday and, it is said, you can see the sun or, in the Christian tradition, angels dancing in a stream or river. At the spring equinox, the sun rises due east and sets due west, giving exactly 12 hours of daylight, and in Christianity the resurrection of Christ is associated with the restoration of light to the world.

A spring equinox ritual for **change and new beginnings**

For this ritual you need two candles: one a bright yellow to represent the growing light, the other slightly shorter in a dark brown or black to represent the receding darkness.

- Light some incense of the spring equinox such as honeysuckle, jasmine or thyme.
- Light next your two candles – the dark one first, followed by the yellow one – saying:

  Light and darkness are no longer equal. The darkness that held me in inaction is now receding. Go, darkness, go.

- Pass the incense nine times anti-clockwise around the dark candle and then nine times around the yellow candle in a clockwise direction, saying:

  Winds of the north retreat, replaced by the keen east winds of change, blowing away inertia and indecision. Out darkness.

- This is one occasion where if you have a candle snuffer it can snuff out the darkness symbolized in the brown or black candle. Equally, you can blow it back to the realms of winter as you extinguish the candle of dark nights.
- Plant a pot of fast-growing seeds or seedlings, this time circling the yellow candle clockwise around it nine times, the number of perfection and completion, saying:

  I have planted the seeds of my endeavour [name it if you wish]. May my new beginnings grow and flourish as the light grows, so that by summer I will have achieved the change that I desire. Grow, light, grow.

- Leave the yellow candle to burn through. Dispose of the dark candle in an environmentally friendly way, as this is not one to use for household light.
- Place your seeds where they can receive sufficient sunlight. Each day as you water your plants, light a yellow candle, saying:

  Grow light grow.

  Then extinguish the candle for use the next day.

- If your seeds or seedlings do not flourish, repeat the ritual as many times as necessary and plant new seedlings. Failure at your first, second or even third attempt does not mean that you will not achieve your new beginning, merely that you may need to be patient and to increase earthly endeavour towards reaching your goal.

Although the most potent spring equinox rituals centre around the three days of the actual festival, you can carry out new beginning rituals at any time during this period using the candle colours of the spring equinox, although you may find these rituals work best during the middle of the waxing moon period and as light floods the sky when dawn heralds a fine day. Use yellow and green for the clear light from the east and the budding vegetation.

Beltain (**Beltane**)

Beltain, from which the modern May Day has grown, ran from sunset on 30 April until sunset on 2 May and marked the beginning of the Celtic summer, when cattle were released from barns and driven between twin fires to cleanse them and to invoke fertility as they were let out into the fields. Young men and girls coupled in the woods and fields on May Eve to bring fertility to the land as well as themselves. The maypole, which symbolized the ancient cosmic tree, formed the focus of fertility dances. Red, blue, green, yellow and white ribbons, representing the union of earth and sky, winter and summer, were entwined.

This is a time that is used for fertility spells, whether for bringing love to fruition, helping a business venture to succeed, or conceiving a child.

A Beltain ritual *for fertility in any aspect of your life*

Eggs are usually associated with the spring equinox and Easter, since painted eggs were offered to the northern spring goddess Ostara. However, they are traditionally a focus for fertility rituals, especially in those cultures where life is seen as coming from the 'cosmic egg'.

You will need as tools a silver knife, a small phial of pure water and a small dish of salt (see Chapter 15 for the significance of these and for more about elemental candles). In this ritual the candles are not lit in the usual clockwise order.

○ Place the salt at the north (12 o'clock) position, the knife at the east (3 o'clock) position, and the water at the west (9 o'clock) position. The candle of the south (see below) forms its own fire elemental substance in this ritual.
○ Take a hen, duck or goose egg

and pierce a small hole in the top so that you can drain out the yolk and white. Carefully split the egg in half, place it in the centre of the circle, and surround it in the four main compass points with four red candles, the colour of passion and fertility as well as Beltain energies.

○ Light first the incense of Beltain (frankincense, lilac or rose) and set it in the Beltain position of south-east (4.30 on a clock face).
○ Light first the candle of the south, saying:

Fire of the south, kindle my fire that I may bring forth the fruit I crave.

○ Drip nine drops of candle wax carefully into the half of the eggshell without the hole, saying:

So do I lay the ground in which my seeds will take root.

○ Light next the candle of the north and sprinkle nine grains of salt into the cooling wax, saying:

Fire of the north, kindle my fire that my seeds may bear fruit.

○ Light next the candle of the east and pierce the wax with the knife, saying:

Fire of the east, fertilize the seeds that they may grow to fruition.

Remove the knife and return it to the 3 o'clock position.

○ Finally, light the candle of the west and add nine drops of water to the mixture, saying:

Fire of the west, nurture my seeds in the waters of the cosmic womb.

○ Cover the egg with the shell and bury it in a secret place.

The energies of the Beltain period last until the summer solstice eve, which is around 21 June, according to the year. Candle fertility rituals are most potent on the three days around Beltain, but you can perform them at any time during this period using the Beltain candle colours. In this case, you should begin your ritual if possible on the full moon at noon, choosing a place in the shadows to light your candles where the sunlight can filter through and add its own fire power. Beltain candle colours are silver and red.

The summer solstice

The longest day falls around 21 June, depending on the year, and is the festival of the full power of the sun. The summer solstice, which begins at dusk on solstice eve and continues for three days, has been celebrated in cultures as far apart as Russian and Native American where sun dances were an assertion of power and courage. Warriors used to attach their chests via cherrywood stakes to a central wheel and dance non-stop for three or four days to bring power and healing to the tribe. The height of the festival is first light on solstice morn, falling like a shaft of gold across standing stones and stone circles, linking the dimensions. The summer solstice is one of the chief festivals of the Druids, who keep watch through solstice eve and continue their celebrations until noon on solstice day.

The Christian festival of midsummer is very close to St John's Day on 24 June. The pagan tradition continued of lighting bonfires on beacon hills to strengthen the power of the sun before it began its decline. Fire wheels were rolled down the

A summer solstice *empowerment spell*

Select a large golden candle, one which will burn for several hours.

- Place your candle in the traditional symbolic due west position. Light it at dusk on the solstice eve or the first day of your spell, saying:

  The light fades, but will return stronger and more golden. Air and fire combine your power in me.

- Next to the candle burn an incense of the solstice: fennel, lavender, rosemary or verbena.
- Let the candle burn until midnight, then light a second long-burning golden candle to add its power at due north, the midnight position. Say:

Though it is the low point of the night, the sun burns still ever stronger and within me too grows the energy to succeed.

- Leave this second candle burning in a safe place, and just before dawn light your third golden candle in the due east position of dawn, saying:

  I greet the dawn of hope on this most golden day. As the sun moves to its height, I draw confidence and strength for my endeavour.

- Watch the sun rise on this most magical day, and as the light floods through surround your

candle with summer flowers.

- Finally, at midday light your fourth golden candle in the south, in the noontide position, and surround its holder with red, green, blue, white and yellow ribbons for the Earth Mother, saying:

  The sun is at its height and I am filled with joy and warmth and light.

- Find an oak tree, tree of the summer solstice, or any large, broad tree and hang your Earth Mother ribbons from it.
- When your fourth candle has burned through, do something practical towards furthering your personal happiness and ambition.

hillsides, flaming tar barrels were swung on chains and blazing torches were tossed in the air.

The summer solstice is the time for rituals for success, power and health, and these are most potent on the three days around the solstice. But its energies last until the eve of Lughnassadh, the first harvest on 31 July, and you can carry out summer solstice rituals using its candle colours at any time in that period, especially at noon, when sunlight and candlelight mingle. For summer solstice candles, use gold or orange to mirror the sun at its height.

Lammas (Lughnassadh)

The festival of the cutting of the corn falls on the eve of 31 July. In the Christian tradition, Lughnassadh has become Lammas, the festival of the first harvest. In Celtic times, it lasted for three days from dusk on 31 July. From the harvesting

---

A Lammas candle ritual for justice

This ritual should be performed in silence until the end.

- Take a single deep purple candle and surround the holder with ears of corn, dried grasses or coarse cream cotton threads. Place a fireproof tray under your candle. Light the candle, focusing on the matter for which you desire justice or an issue on which you have been unfairly treated.
- By candlelight, plait the corn or grasses into several segments, perhaps one for each injustice or specific delay, endowing the thickening strands with all the frustration, delays and procrastination. Return them to their circle around the candle.
- In the Lammas position of south-west light the incense of Lammas, which includes copal, ferns, heather and sandalwood.
- On the plaited grasses around the candle, place at the eight main compass points of the wheel of the year (the last two are Hallowe'en in the north-west and the midwinter solstice in the

north) eight hazelnuts. Begin at the Lammas position and proceed clockwise. A ninth should be set directly in front of the south position.

Hazel is the Celtic tree of wisdom, especially during the season when it brings forth nuts, symbolic of kernels of wise thoughts. It is associated with the sacred number nine, since the hazel takes nine years to produce nuts and because there was a sacred well called Connla's Well in Tipperary, Ireland, over which hung the nine hazels of poetic art.

The Druids carried a hazel rod as a symbol of authority. In ancient courts, a hazel rod was held by the accused to ensure a fair hearing. Hazel was also used to mark the boundaries of a court of justice and so it can also represent boundaries as a subsidiary meaning.

So, while other nuts can be used for this spell, the hazel is special.

- As you set each nut, visualize a step forward in your life. Take your time and let the answers flow from your inner untapped well of

inspiration, from the kernels of Connla's Well, of which these are symbols.
- When the nuts are in place, pick up the nearest strand of corn or thread to the Lammas position. Set it alight in the flame and drop it on the tray to burn away. As you do so, see a delay or frustration being cleared. Continue to burn the strands from an anti-clockwise direction, seeing the knots of officialdom untangling, so that by the time you return to Lammas the problems have been cleared.
- Blow out the candle, speaking for the first time:

  Let justice be done. I rest my case.

  Avoid thinking about or acting on the issue for a full night and day if possible, and you will find a fresh perspective.

- Keep your nuts in a red bag and (if you do not have a nut allergy) eat one each evening at dusk, absorbing in the old magical tradition the wisdom of the Druids.

of the corn came the first loaf, hence in some churches this is still offered on the altar on 2 August, the day whose medieval name was Loaf Mass. The last sheaf of corn was believed to contain the spirit of the corn god, so it was cut by a number of people casting their sickles; then no one would know who had cut down the corn god, who offered himself willingly so that there would be good future harvests and was reborn at the midwinter solstice to the Earth Mother.

As well as being used to make the harvest loaf, some of the corn was made into corn dollies, symbol of the Earth Mother, decorated with the scarlet ribbons of Frigg, the Norse mother goddess. These corn dollies would be hung over domestic hearths throughout winter.

The old name for this month in the Celtic Coligny calendar was Claimtime, when debts would be collected and justice dispensed, as the tracks were dry enough for the judges (originally the Druids) to travel. Contracts were arranged and trial marriages, for a year and a day, were frequently set up at Lammas, with a young couple joining hands through a holed stone.

Lammas is potent for rituals concerning justice, rights, contracts, business affairs, commitments and partnerships of all kinds. Its energies persist until the autumn equinox around 22 September. But you can carry out justice candle rituals at any time using the candles colours of Lammas, in which case you should begin your ritual as the full moon begins to wane. For Lammas, use dark orange and yellow candles to reflect the coming of autumn, and purple for justice.

The autumn equinox

This falls around 22 September, according to the year, and is the festival of reaping what you have sown. The autumn equinox, the second time of the balance between day and night in the wheel of the year, runs for three days from dusk on the equinox eve and marks the beginning of longer nights. In the story of the year, the god of light is defeated by his twin and alter-ego, the god of darkness.

This second 'wild' or 'green' harvest was a time of celebration for the fruits and vegetables of the earth and the Earth Mother. This is the time of the second harvest of vegetables, fruit and remaining crops, the 'harvest home'. The harvest supper pre-dates Christianity. On the day when equal night and day heralded winter, the feast formed a sympathetic magical gesture to ensure that there would be enough food during the winter, by displaying and consuming the finest of the harvest. It is also a time when in the older religions the sky and animal god is said to retreat for the long winter. Druids climb to the top of a hill to take leave of the summer sun as the nights will get longer.

Michaelmas – the day of St Michael, the archangel of the sun – was celebrated on 29 September with a feast centred around a goose. Since St Michael was patron saint of high places and replaced the pagan sun deities, he was an apt symbol for the last days of the summer sun.

The three days around the autumn equinox are, then, a time for rituals concerning the completion of any unfinished tasks, the ending of quarrels and the setting down of unresolved anger. But its energies last until Samhain or

An autumnal ritual to **complete a task**

- Beginning in the west, place eight small green candles in a circle at the compass points, and four larger blue candles in a circle outside at the four main compass points, again beginning in the west.
- Before you light the candles, burn in the west of the circle some incense of the autumn equinox – which includes ferns, geranium, myrrh and pine – and focus on what it is you need to complete or achieve.
- Light first the inner circle of candles, beginning in the west and moving clockwise, saying:

  This is my completed task waiting only to be manifest in the outer world.

- Light next the blue candle in the west and circle it with pins, saying:

  This is the confidence in myself I need to believe I can succeed.

- Ignite next the candle in the north and scatter pins around it, saying:

  These are the practical skills and persistence I need to complete this task competently.

- Burn next the candle in the east, scattering pins and saying:

  This is the logic, the focus and the determination to overcome any obstacles.

- Light the final candle in the south and scatter the pins, saying:

  This is the energy and the action to make a supreme effort to complete my goal.

- In the same order, use a magnet or lodestone to pick up each circle of pins, saying for the first:

  So do I overcome fear of failure and inadequacy in myself and my abilities.

  Blow out the candle in the west.

- Collect your pins in a small square box.
- Pick up the second circle of pins, saying:

  So can I find practical solutions to any obstacles in my way.

  Blow out the candle of the north.

- Pick up the third circle of pins, saying:

  So can I overcome indecision and muddled thinking.

  Blow out the candle in the east.

- Collect the fourth circle of pins, saying:

  So do I overcome inertia, inaction and loss of my earlier inspiration.

  Blow out the candle in the south.

- Put the lid on the box of pins and keep it in a drawer until the task is complete.
- Sit down by the light of your small circle of candles and list the steps you need to finish the task and the time you will take for each.
- Let this circle burn down while you take the first step on your list.

Hallowe'en on 31 October, and you can carry out completion rituals at any time during the year using the candle colours of the autumn equinox. Such spells are best carried out, not as you might expect during the waning moon period, but on the full moon, because in these rituals you need a surge of power to finish the race or mend a relationship. For autumn equinox candles, use blue for the autumn rain and green for the Earth Mother and the wild harvest.

Samhain

This falls on 31 October and is a festival for facing and overcoming fears. I have already described it in Chapter 3 and suggested a Day of the Dead ritual.

Samhain, known in the modern world as Hallowe'en, the beginning of the Celtic year and a time for welcoming home family ghosts, runs from sunset on 31 October for three days and incorporates the Christian Days of the Dead, All Souls' Day and All Saints' Day. It was the time when the cattle were brought from the hills for the winter and either put in byres or slaughtered for meat, having been driven through twin fires to purify them. These fires also served to drive away bad spirits who were believed to lurk at the transition of the year, as well as to light

OPPOSITE Like the ancient wishing-well offerings, money spells can attract prosperity.

A Samhain ritual for overcoming **a lingering fear**

Some of our fears stem from childhood or adolescence and have root in a real unhappiness or misfortune. But over the years these hidden worries can become detached from the original cause, so that we may fear travelling by plane, being in a dark place or even being left alone. Psychoanalysts may uncover these root causes, while cognitive psychologists adjust patterns of behaviour without seeking out origins. This spell can help to heal life fears without painful probing. It seems to touch a deep part of our psyche. This ritual also works for deep-seated sorrows and regrets.

- In your bathroom, light the incense of Samhain: cedar, cypress, dittany, ferns or sage.
- Next, light three large navy blue candles. Add to your bath just two or three drops of a gentle protective oil such as rose or geranium. Sit in your bath in the candlelight and watch the candles casting light on the water.
- Take a jar of herbal bath salts in either lavender, sandalwood or frankincense. These fragrances are widely available in both supermarkets and pharmacies. Take a few grains of the salts and cast them into a pool of light in the water, saying:

  Darkness to light, come out of the corners and flee.

- Stir the pool of light until the salt dissolves, saying:

  Melt away you who have lingered too long in the shadows of my soul.

- Repeat this five times and then get out of the bath and pull out the plug. Watch the water flow away carrying your fear, while reciting:

  Fears without name, flow from me, like the rivers to the sea. Pain and hurt, wash far, be gone, lingering terror is there none.

- Let your candles burn away naturally.

home both living and deceased family members. There have always been fears of the unknown focused around this festival, anxieties that our ancestors projected on to witches and malevolent fairies, who might be kept away by the Jack o'Lantern – a candle in a turnip.

The three days around Samhain are therefore potent for rituals for protection, overcoming fears, laying old ghosts (psychological as well as psychic), and for marking the natural transition between one stage of life and the next. These energies continue until the midwinter solstice around 21 December, but you can carry out protective rituals at any time using the candle colours of Samhain. The later part of the waning moon cycle is ideal for these. For Samhain, use black, navy blue or deep purple candles for letting go of fear, and orange for the joy of immortality that is promised at this time.

The midwinter **solstice**

This falls around 21 December, according to the year, and is a festival of hope. The midwinter solstice or shortest day, the forerunner of Christmas, runs from the eve of the shortest day for three days and is a time for welcoming the rebirth of the sun. Its origins lie before recorded history, when the early peoples lit bonfires as a magical gesture to persuade the sun to shine again. In Chapter 2, I described the solstice candle and suggested it could become a focus for quiet celebration at a time when tempers can be frayed and goodwill jaded in the run-up to the modern Christmas festival.

Our present festival is a glorious amalgamation of many ancient festivals that centred around the midwinter solstice – Norse, Celtic, Mithraic, Greek and Roman – as well as Christian celebrations. The common theme is that the sun itself, the sun god or Son of God is reborn at the darkest hour of the year and life begins again. And so candles are a special way of creating light from darkness, warmth amid ice and snow, and abundance at a time when food was in short supply. The feasting of Christmas was another magical gesture to ensure that there would be food again in spring and good harvests the following year.

The three days around the solstice are a good time for prosperity and money spells, as well as abundance in less material ways. But the winter solstice energies extend until the eve of Brigantia on 30 January, and you can carry out this or a similar prosperity ritual at any time, using the candle colours of the midwinter solstice. In this case, the crescent moon – when traditionally we turn over our silver three times and bow to the moon – is best for spells concerning increase. For the midwinter solstice, use white, scarlet, brilliant green and gold candles.

A *midwinter* money spell

- Collect as many coins as you can – they need not be of any particular denomination – and place them in a clear glass or crystal jar. There is usually an amazing amount of loose change left lying around the average family home!
- Collect a second smaller pot of money; this one should be of pottery and have a lid. Here we are following the tradition of the American Midwest copper jars that would be kept in family kitchens to attract wealth to the household.
- Find as many candles as you can. This is a good opportunity to use candles left over from other rituals, as long as these were for increase and attraction spells and not banishing ones. If you prefer not to carry out the spell with used candles or you need more, choose red and white household candles. Arrange your candles in any way you wish and use jars and bottles if you run out of holders.

- Place your white or gold solstice candle – which should be as large as you can afford – behind the clear money jar, so that when it is illuminated it will shine on the coins.
- Light incense of the midwinter (bay, cedar, juniper or rosemary) and a small white taper candle. If you are carrying out the ritual on the solstice eve, wait until dusk to light this candle.
- Ignite your solstice candle and circle it with coins from your lidded pot.
- Now begin illuminating your candles one by one in random order, taking a coin from the lidded jar and setting it in front of each candle so that the light will shine upon it. When all your candles are ablaze, sit in the bright candlelight, watching the flames glinting on the coins. Say:

Light of the sun, increase what now I have, so that I may have sufficient and a little more for myself and the needs of my loved ones. Money grow and increase with the sun and moon.

- When it is quite dark, extinguish the candles one by one, returning the coins to the pottery jar. Leave only the solstice candle burning in a safe place.
- When light breaks through, put the coins around the solstice candle into the lidded pottery jar once more.
- Leave both jars in a warm place for a full moon cycle and give the money in the crystal jar to a good cause.
- Spend the contents of the smaller pot of money on something for the home or the ingredients for a family meal.
- Continue your money jar collections; give the larger one to charity and you will find your fortunes may prosper in a far greater proportion to your efforts than you would expect.

The wheel of the year: *a candle ritual of personal integration*

You may wish to carry out this ritual with a friend or friends, but you can perform it equally well alone.

○ Set eight festival candles in the different colours from the wheel of the year, beginning with the period in which your birthday falls. As there is some overlap of colours, the ones suggested below ensure a different colour for each segment. Make the wheel large enough to walk around the inside without catching your skin or clothing on the burning candles, and also so that you can enter at your birth point. If you are working with friends they too can enter at their own seasonal point.

○ Set at each point a living symbol of the period that contains *prana* or the life force, so that your wheel links growth in the natural world with your personal growth. At the end of the description of the ritual I have listed some suggestions for seasonal flowers and fruit. Make sure there is one edible item at each focal point, so that you can follow the old magical action of eating the strengths of the season.

○ Enter the circle and light your birth season candle, repeating its energy word three times, a sacred number of growth. For example, for Beltain the word is 'fertility'.

○ At this point, sit or kneel facing the candle and concentrate on areas of your life or specific needs where you require the energies symbolized by the festival candle – for example, fertility or fresh input at Beltain.

○ When you are ready, eat or drink a symbol of that particular festival energy, saying:

I take into myself the strengths of this time, that my life may move forward with the natural cycles of the seasons.

○ When you have lit all the candles, walk clockwise around the outside of the circle, saying:

Wheel turn, candles burn, that my life may be whole and complete and in tune with the natural rhythms of the earth.

○ Enter the circle again and stand in front of the festival point that falls immediately before your birth date period. Blow out this candle and continue anti-clockwise around the circle, extinguishing each candle in turn, ending with your own birth festival candle.

○ Do not speak while you are walking, but name in your mind the attributes of the festivals, and when you have circled your own candle, say:

Light to darkness, darkness to light, so the world turns. Each season brings its own strength and I rejoice that I hold all within me.'

Brigantia: north-east
Focus New love and trust.
Symbol The first snowdrops or very early budding leaves or flowers, milk, cream or edible seeds.
Light a pink candle.

The spring equinox: due east
Focus Change, new beginnings.
Symbol Any spring flowers, leaves in bud or a sprouting pot of seeds, for example crocuses, daffodils, primroses, snowdrops or violets. A small chocolate rabbit.
Light a yellow candle.

Beltain: south-east
Focus Fertility.
Symbol Fresh greenery, especially hawthorn (indoors only on 1 May); any flowers that are native to your region, placed in baskets, eggs. A sweet egg.
Light a red candle.

The summer solstice: due south
Focus Success, happiness, health.
Symbol Summer flowers, oak boughs, St John's wort (hypericum), the herb of midsummer, or golden fern pollen that is said to reveal buried treasure wherever it falls. A peach or summer fruit.
Light a gold candle.

Lammas: south-west
Focus Justice and commitments.
Symbol Corn ears, wheat, cereals, hazel nuts, poppies and cornflowers.
Light a purple candle.

The autumn equinox: due west
Focus Completion and reconciliation.
Symbol Russet, yellow or orange leaves, willow boughs, harvest fruits such as apples and pears, and autumn green, yellow and red vegetables. Berries.
Light a blue candle.

Samhain: north-west
Focus Banishing fears.
Symbol Apples, which are a symbol of health and which feature in the Hallowe'en game of love divination, an ancient custom dating from Druidic times, pumpkins, nuts and autumn leaves, mingled with evergreens as a mystic promise that life continues on its way.
Light an orange candle.

The midwinter solstice: due north
Focus Promises of future happiness, healing.
Symbol Evergreen boughs, especially pine or fir, holly, small logs of wood, especially oak and ash (sacred trees in northern mythology) found naturally rather than cut. A dish of cooked root vegetables or a seasonal food such as Christmas pudding.
Light a white candle.

Candle Magic for All Occasions

Candle magic can be as simple or as elaborate as you wish. It can be divided into attracting magic, for bringing something that is lacking into your life, and banishing magic, for removing from your life what it is you no longer need or which is proving destructive. The rituals in this chapter are just suggestions and you can create your own spells and empowerments, using the associations given in this book for candle colours, fragrances and so on, above all adding the most powerful words of all – those from the heart.

All you need for basic candle magic is a single candle in an appropriate colour, or a light or white candle for any attracting magic and a dark-coloured one for banishing magic.

A simple candle attraction ritual for a **new job or promotion**

For this ritual, use a pure white candle, or an orange one if the job is creative or involves dealing with people, or a yellow one if it involves logic, business or the media. Predominantly practical jobs can be represented by brown.

○ Before you light the candle, sit quietly and focus on your specific need. Write on paper or in your mind an advertisement for the precise job, ideal salary and conditions. Although it may be easier and seem better to be open about the kind of work you would be prepared to accept, for purposes of focus and concentration more psychic energy is generated within narrow parameters.

Alternatively, you can cut from the newspaper either the advertisement for the job for which you intend to apply, or one very similar to the one to which you hope to be promoted. Read this until you have memorized it.

○ If you are job-hunting, you can carry out rituals for more than one job, as long as you can summon the same intensity of feeling for each post.

○ Rub oil into the candle: either pure olive oil or a candle oil containing cinnamon, patchouli or peppermint. See the candle as a magnet and move upwards from the centre to the north pole and then downwards to the south; as you do so, repeat a mantra or chant over and over again in a monotone, such as:

Staff Nurse on Wilmington Hospital Children's Ward.

or

An extra £2,000 a year salary.

Endow the candle mentally with these words as though you were etching them with an awl and see them burned in the candle.

○ When you are ready, light the candle and look into the flame, not only visualizing the moment when you are offered the job or increased salary, but hearing the words, feeling the handshake and your satisfaction, even perhaps smelling the particular fragrances of the workplace. The more multi-sensory a visualization, the more powerful it is.

○ Run through the experience in increasing detail two or three times and then blow out the candle, sending the power in the direction of your anticipated workplace.

○ Repeat this ritual whenever it is necessary – particularly if you are in the position of having suffered a rebuff or need a boost to your confidence.

Banishing *candle rituals*

The following is a simple candle ritual to overcome an obstacle. It may be that you want to move house and have found just the place, but your own house is not selling, although you have reduced the price and similar properties are selling in your area. Or you want to study for an important exam, but minor crises demand your time. Below you can see how Ginny carried out such a spell.

Ginny's candle ritual **to leave home**

Ginny was 25 and had moved back home two years earlier after her father had died suddenly. Her mother was in excellent health, financially secure and had a wide circle of friends and interests, but every time Ginny suggested moving back to her own flat, which she had temporarily rented to a friend, her mother put an obstacle in the way. Ginny's job was located near her flat 50km (30 miles) away and the daily round trip to work was proving a strain. She was also missing her freedom and friends, but every time the move was planned, her mother became ill, someone she knew was burgled, there was a problem with the house or she would resort to tears and threats of suicide.

Things came to a head when Ginny's friend gave a month's notice and she needed to find another, more permanent tenant quickly – or move back herself.

○ Ginny lit a dark grey pillar candle, on which she etched halfway down the symbol of Saturn (see Chapter 8), the planet of limitations and endings. She began her ritual on Saturn's hour, the third hour after sunset, in the evening on Saturday, the day of Saturn.

○ Ginny looked into the flame and said:

As this candle burns away, so will the ties of guilt and my mother's possessiveness diminish, leaving only love.

○ She watched the candle until the Saturn symbol had burned away. Then she blew it out, blowing away with it the obstacles to her freedom. When the candle was cool, she wrapped the remains in dark silk, to be re-lit whenever her resolve wavered.

○ Ginny repeated the ritual on two consecutive Saturdays with new grey candles, burning the remaining candle each time in midweek just before she broached the subject of moving out to her mother.

○ On the fourth Saturday, Ginny ignored her mother's impending migraine and moved back to her own flat. When she phoned home the next day, her mother was entertaining friends and soon afterwards booked a holiday with them, on which she met a widower with similar interests to her own. Ginny's candle ritual had, ironically, freed them both.

Candle magic on the **new moon**

One of the most beautiful informal candle rituals that can be carried out either alone or with a group of friends is a wishes ceremony on the new moon, a day or two before you can see the crescent in the sky or, more usually, the day of the visible crescent moon. The new moon is very magical, especially if the night is clear and you can leave the curtains open, so that the crescent is a symbol of hope.

If you want to make this a monthly event, either set up a communal fund to pay for candles and oils or take turns at hosting the event. You can, however, have a really beautiful ceremony by yourself.

Preparing for candle magic

- Clear any furniture back against the wall and set cushions in a circle around the floor. Decorate the room with a few silver candles for the moon, so that you will not need artificial light. Play some gentle music as background. Light incense sticks of jasmine and myrrh for the moon.
- You will need candles for everyone's zodiac colour and one for their most pressing need or wish (see Chapter 4 for both zodiacal and wish colours). Of course, you might end up with six Librans and so need six blue or lilac candles, and another six people with wishes relating to blue candles – for justice, travel and success, to name but three. It is better to overstock for these occasions rather than be caught out. Remember, however, that you can always use white candles as a substitute for any other colour.
- Old bottles and jars can serve as candle holders if you run out, although many people like to bring their own special holders. Place the candle-anointing oils in small dishes, using lunar oils such as clary sage, jasmine, lemon, myrrh, neroli and ylang ylang, and add dishes of tapers and maybe a large central flame from which candles and tapers can be lit.
- If you are expecting a group of people, choose one person in advance to make sure that everyone has what they need, and to advise on candle colours and ways of anointing candles for people who have never before used candles for magic.
- Provide also a selection of different-coloured strips of paper and a supply of pens on which to write wishes. You will need a dish or small tray under the wish candle to catch the ashes of the wish.
- Ask those who are coming to bring symbols to set around the candles, such as jewellery and coins for prosperity, flowers for love, fruit for health and golden objects or charms for success. Small silver objects symbolize the moon, for silver is both the colour and metal of the moon. Candlesticks in a silver colour are also symbolic.
- Red, yellow and orange crystals or glass nuggets, for abundance and prosperity, can be added to circle the candles, plus moonstones for moon magic.

Beginning candle magic

When people arrive, they can sit in the circle with their zodiacal and wish candles, anointing them and focusing on their particular hopes for the coming months.

- The oil should be applied first to the astrological candle and then to the candle of need, while visualizing the most pressing need or wish coming to fruition. Each person's candles can be lit when ready, with the astrological candle first. Then write the wish on a strip of paper in the same colour as the candle of need.
- Begin the actual ceremony by invoking protection, perhaps by lighting the four elemental candles in the four quadrants of the room, beginning with the green candle in the north to invoke the archangels (see Chapter 15). Alternatively, you can ask for light and protection on the group and let everyone send light from their candles to enclose the group in a beautiful circle of gold. Personal,

Attracting a new partner or *strengthening an existing relationship*

This ritual is more complex only in that you may use more tools, add more stages, extend the time and perhaps begin the spell on a particular day, lunar phase or hour. Of all the love rituals I have suggested and used, those with candles and mirrors are perhaps the most effective, since you can draw the love into the mirror. There are many variations – this is just one of them.

Since this is a ritual for attracting love, which is associated with Venus and the increasing power of the moon, a good time to carry out the spell would be the three nights before the full moon. Alternatively, you could begin the spell on a Friday, the day of Venus, and perhaps use the hour of Venus on each of the three days (see table in Chapter 8). After sunset is good, but in winter you could also use the hours of darkness before dawn.

A large gold or silver oval mirror is best for this kind of magic. You can buy gilt ones quite cheaply, or get an old one from a car boot sale and clean and repaint it.

If you are strengthening an existing love, use your own and your lover's birth candle colours. If you are seeking a partner, take your own birth candle and one in pink for a woman or green for a man. Use tall, slender candles.

Place the lover candles – yours plus his or hers – one on either side of the mirror. Put your birth candle to the left and your lover's or projected lover's to the right, so that both can be seen in the mirror.

The first night

○ First light a horseshoe of six alternate pink and green candles, the number of Venus, beginning from the right with pink if you are female. These should not be tall enough to be seen directly in the mirror, but will cast a glow on the glass. Place the small candles on a fireproof tray so that their melting wax can mingle, and so that they frame the love candles and the mirror.

○ Sit in the candlelight and watch the light flickering on the mirror, as it does so whispering:

Come love to me.

or

Grow love and flow.

○ Encircle the mirror and candles with a ring of tiny pink rose quartz and soft green jade, the crystals of Venus and love, or use pink and green glass nuggets if you do not have any crystals, saying:

So I call/encircle my loved one and he/she encircles me so that we will be/are closer bound in love, trust and fidelity, so long as we both desire.

○ Light your own candle first and then the second candle of love, calling softly to an unknown person who would make you happy or naming an existing partner:

May the fire of love so be kindled between us.

As you speak these words, carefully move the two candles slightly closer together and look into the mirror, so that you can see your own image in the near right corner, framed in light.

○ Draw your lover towards you in the glass by visualizing a figure coming from the far corner of the mirror and moving closer. You may see a faint image in the glass over your shoulder or in your mind's vision, but if not, greet once more your unknown or known love, asking that he or she may move closer over the ensuing days. Do not turn around.

○ Blow out the tall candles together if possible, but if not, in the reverse order of lighting, sending the love to wherever your lover is, asking him or her to send love in return. You may see the other person more clearly in the after-image.

spontaneous words are far more potent than those that are prepared in advance, and in candlelight it is easy to speak from the depths of your soul.

○ A few minutes of silence and stillness can then follow, with the candlelight glinting on the crystals, coins and symbols of abundance, while you all visualize a happier future and tune in to the new moon energies, which promise new beginnings.

○ After this, one of the group can begin a guided visualization of abundance, perhaps invoking such ideas as golden coins showering down from a golden horn, flowers blossoming and bringing health and new life, ice melting and

- Leave the small candles burning a few moments longer and sit quietly in the light, perhaps hearing words or seeing pictures in your mind or in the mirror. Blow out these candles also in the reverse order that you lit them.

The second night

- On the second night, at the hour of Venus, relight the candles, first the horseshoe, beginning from the left, then your lover's and finally your own candle.
- Repeat the ritual and words, bringing the two tall candles even closer together, saying as you do so either personal words of love or:

  My true love has my heart and I have his/hers.

- This time, the image in the mirror may be much closer so that you feel you could almost touch, but again do not turn around. If you smile, you may see the other person smiling too. Do not be surprised if you recognize the other person, as we may work or see someone every day and only suddenly see them through the eyes of love, as though it were the most natural thing in the world. As you look at the image, you may hear as a whisper words of love returning in your mind's ear. These may be the first words your lover says when you meet for the first time or after an absence.

- Once again, blow out the candles, first yours and then that of the loved one. See the light in long, thin rays bound off the mirror and disappear into the darkness.
- As before, sit by the light of your small candles. By now your wax may be forming a distinctive shape, an image that may tell you how love will come or how it will develop.
- Before blowing out each tiny candle in the reverse order that you lit them, recite again:

  My true love has my heart and I have his/hers.

The third night

- On the third night, at the hour of Venus, in front of your hoop of small candles place a book open at your favourite love poem, with a gold-coloured ring in the centre and a sprig of ivy or myrtle, both signs of fidelity. Alternatively, follow the age-old love tradition of placing a ring on a prayer book opened at the marriage service, a practice which even if you do not want to get married has traditionally been a sign of spiritual as well as physical love.
- This time, light your horseshoe of candles from right to left, then your candle and finally your lover's, saying:

  Love to light, light to love, join our hearts you powers above.

- Move the two tall candles so that they touch and pass the ring through the flame of each, saying:

  With this ring I thee wed.

- Split the myrtle or ivy in half and, making sure your candles and holders are on a fireproof surface, burn half the sprig of ivy or myrtle in each, saying:

  Faithful unto thee, faithful unto me.

- Only now look into the mirror over the candles and see your face and that of the other close in the two flames, becoming one. The figure may be at your side and you may even feel a light touch on your hand and shoulder, but continue looking straight ahead.
- Let all the candles burn away naturally. Look for another sign in the mingled wax of the small candles, and when it is cool draw a heart with your joint initials entwined, or yours and a question mark inside if the lover is unknown.
- You can, if you wish, keep the heart in a silk scarf in a drawer. Otherwise, bury it in a deep pot and on top plant flowers of love or herbs: basil for attracting love, forget-me-nots for undying love, lavender for gentleness, marigolds for enduring feelings or parsley for fertility and passion. Concentrate on making other aspects of your life happy and love will come and grow when the time is right.

water flowing. Everyone can then contribute an idea of their own to the shower of wishes in turn: they may speak of a new house, travel, love, success at work, the restoration of the health of self or a loved one, the mending of a quarrel or perhaps the flowering of new trust. This is optional, and some people prefer to maintain the silence.

- At a given signal, begin one at a time around the circle burning each wish, lighting the paper from the astrological candle and burning it in the candle of need. As each wish is burned, everyone present should send love and positive thoughts to carry the wish on its way.

Reducing the power of **an addiction or compulsion**

Candle magic is a very gentle way of loosening the ties that bind people to destructive habits, whether it be smoking or drinking too much, excessive eating, dieting or even exercising, so that pleasure becomes obsession. It replaces the urgency with a soft, healing light that absorbs not only the compulsion, but the inner pain that may be causing the need to over-compensate the body.

○ Begin on a Monday, on a day of the waning moon at dawn, with a large red pillar candle that represents the natural physical drives which have gone into overload. As you sit in the decreasing darkness, let all your anxieties and inwardly directed destructive urges flow away, saying:

Leave me, flow, go away and be cooled. Lose your power to drive me on a downward path and let there be peace within me.

○ Set a soft grey candle to absorb the pain and urgency where the dawn of new beginnings can flood on it. Light the red candle first, then the grey. As you do so, visualize the red raw energies flowing into the softer candle, where they are absorbed and cooled. Sit until almost the end of the moon's hour, feeling the heat leaving you and gently cooling energies entering.

○ At the end of the hour after dawn, drip wax from the scarlet candle in a metal bucket or deep bowl of cold water, standing back so that the hot wax does not splash you, and let it harden on the water to form an image to guide you.

○ Dowse the red candle in the bucket, saying:

Be gone from me, power to burn, power to drive me against my will.

Let the grey candle burn out naturally in the growing light.

○ If it is not raining, go out into the open air, remove and dispose of any fragments of red candle and wax, and tip the water away down a drain, letting go of any vestiges of compulsion and feeling the promises of new life stirring.

○ Repeat the ritual every Monday at dawn whenever possible, for as long as necessary. If dawn is not convenient, carry out the ritual when you have the time, ideally once a week.

○ Be kind to yourself and do not expect miracles. Addictions build up over years and each small step is a victory of which you should be proud.

○ In time, use a smaller red candle and a correspondingly larger grey one, until at last there is only a grey candle remaining.

Closing the ceremony

○ When all the wishes have been burned, a designated person should close down the circle either by thanking the archangels and extinguishing the elemental candles, beginning this time with the blue candle in the west, or asking the participants to draw back the protective light into their own candles.

○ Leave the candles to burn away in a safe place on a tray, while you have supper by candlelight. Rather than preparing it in advance, let everyone bring something for a shared meal and get it ready together – an excellent grounding process and drawing-together of the strands of the evening.

Health-giving rituals help replace an unhealthy lifestyle with a more positive attitude.

PART THREE *Candles and*
Psychic Development

CHAPTER ELEVEN

Candles and Meditation

Candles offer a natural focus for psychic work. Gazing into a candle flame is the simplest and yet perhaps most spiritual form of meditation, and in the altered state of consciousness you may uncover, quite spontaneously, strategies and solutions to even seemingly insurmountable obstacles, by tapping into the natural intuitive wisdom that lies beneath conscious thought and anxieties.

The act of lighting a candle at dusk and sitting in the growing darkness provides an escape from the material world and has a timeless quality that can dissolve the barriers of time and space. Anyone who has fallen into a reverie while sitting in candlelight has entered a spontaneous natural meditative state.

Candle meditation involves focusing on the flame, excluding conscious thoughts and actions, allowing your unconscious mind to work without distraction and your psyche to carry you where it will. Meditation in the evening will banish the stresses of the day and still racing thoughts, so that you are left relaxed and sleepy, allowing your mind to work creatively through your dreams, so that you wake refreshed and inspired.

You should experiment with different candle sizes, colours and formations, from a single candle to a circle of candles surrounding a large crystal. Purple or silver are often used, but your own meditative colour may be rich scarlet or gold.

Scented candles are evocative for meditation, especially lavender, pine or sandalwood (see Chapter 5). You can also surround your candle with fragrant flowers or herbs.

You may wish sometimes to use a mantra, or power word, spoken softly and repetitively in a monotone, as you look into the flame. The most basic and commonly used power word in meditative chanting is *Om* or *Aum*, said to be the sound of the universe that brought it into being; however, you can use any rhythmic, resounding word as a focus.

One effect of meditation is a heightened state of awareness and one in which all the senses merge quite naturally. Colours may seem brighter, fragrance overpowering and sounds not only heightened but transmuted, so that the distant roar of cars may become a waterfall, a ringing telephone the sound of church bells. The images evoked are usually symbols that you have experienced in dreams or that are meaningful to you, and may hold keys to your future paths.

Past-life work, astral projection and divination, which are described in the following chapters, can all begin with the act of lighting a candle and then letting the feelings and images flow.

Beginning **meditation**

Find a quiet, safe place for meditation where you will not be disturbed. Sleep is a common result of meditation, so ensure that your candle cannot be knocked over and that there is no chance of fire should you drift off. A candle in an enclosed glass holder, a night light in a lantern or a large candle floating on a bowl of water, are safe foci.

If you are seeking inspiration or an answer that is eluding you, carry out your candle meditation at dusk, the traditional transition time between day and night. Choose a time when you are not too tired, have a bath in a gentle fragrance such as geranium or chamomile, and follow this with a very light meal or warm drink.

- Wear something loose and light, and sit where you can gaze into the candle flame safely.
- Place both feet flat on the floor; if you wish, support your back with a pillow and have arm rests on the chair for your elbows. Sit up straight without straining your muscles. In the sitting position, you should have your arms resting comfortably in your lap with palms upwards. Some people prefer to sit cross-legged on the floor with their hands supporting their knees.
- Aim initially for 5, then 10 minutes of meditation, building up to 20–30 minutes – but be ruled by your own needs. Do not fight the sensation of the outer world returning, even if this happens before you had expected your meditation to end: this means your psyche has done its work.
- Place the candle so that you can see it without moving your neck or head. Experiment with different heights of table and distances until you feel comfortable.

Breathing in the light
- See yourself surrounded by a circle of warm, protective light emanating from your candle. Let this circle expand until you are bathed in it, but can see quite clearly through it to the candle flame.
- Concentrate on breathing, slowly and deeply. Take a slow, deep breath through your nose, hold it for one and two and three, then slowly exhale through your mouth.
- As you inhale, visualize the golden candlelight entering your body and dark light leaving. Continue until you see only the golden light being inhaled and exhaled, and your breathing is slow and steady.

Entering the light
- Become your breathing and do not attempt to move beyond it, remaining focused on the candle flame but not attempting to see any pictures in it, although some people report seeing sparks emanating from the candle at this stage. This aura becomes visible as you trust your psychic sight.

- Feel the golden light permeating first your toes and feet, then your legs, your body, arms, fingers, neck and head, until you are totally immersed and completely relaxed.

- Now let the candle flame expand and fill your mind, so that all other sights, sounds and sensations merge and recede. Let the warm light swirl from without and within, enfolding you and merging with you as you inhale, like waves ebbing and flowing. Allow any words and pictures also to come and go without attempting to hold or analyse them.

- Gradually move away from the focus, connecting with your breathing once more and letting the light also fade. As you do this, external sounds will return and your normal range of vision expand until you are fully aware once more.

- Stretch like a cat, slowly and luxuriantly, and spend the time before sleep listening to soothing music or sitting as the candle burns down, dreaming of golden shores and moonlit mountains.

- If you had any inspirations or images during your meditation, record them in words or pictures.

- If the candle is still burning at bedtime, blow it out, sending the light to anyone you know who is ill or lonely, and see if the fallen wax has created an image that may offer you an extra insight.

A candle and **crystal meditation**

Crystals with candlelight shining on them form a powerful focus for meditation (see also Chapter 13). The energies of the crystal are like the candle itself, composed of the ancient elements of earth, air, fire and water, the volcanic eruptions, the erosion by air and water that created these beautiful crystals during their millennia in the rocks.

- Light a clear white candle and surround it with sparkling or transparent stones such as clear crystal quartz, purple amethysts, yellow citrine, pink rose quartz and the translucent brown tiger's eye and moonstones that range in colour from creamy white, through yellow to blue.

  Alternatively, you can use a crystal sphere or ball. These come not only in clear quartz but also in blue beryl, polished amethyst and rose quartz.

Caithness paperweights make excellent foci for candle meditation; try also opaque agate eggs that will reflect the flame and cast shadows in the quartz.

- You can either ring your candle with nine smaller crystals of any of the above, or place your candle behind a single large agate or marble egg or a crystalline sphere so that the light reflects in it. In either case, concentrate on the candle flame primarily and let the crystal lights join with it.

  In Chapter 13 I describe the technique of candle scrying, where you gaze into a mirror or crystal ball and look for pictures, perhaps to answer a specific question. Because meditation is more open-ended than scrying, you clear your mind of questions and if images come into your mind or the flame, they are

valuable by-products. That said, many people do discover spontaneous clairvoyant powers in candle meditation. Second sight is not a spooky power possessed only by a few gifted psychics, but a widespread ability, an extension of physical sight that is simply not used in so-called developed society, where we rely on technology to interpret and communicate. How pleasant it would be to replace the noises of the modern world, such as the mobile phone, with telepathy.

- As with simple candle meditation, begin by breathing slowly and deeply. You may find that the crystal colours appear to form rainbow breath or combine to produce pure white light to be inhaled. This is pure *prana*, the life force, and will leave you feeling renewed and at peace with the rest of the world.

Cindy's candle **meditation**

Cindy had been offered a large loan by her bank to pay off existing commitments that were proving a serious drain on her business. Yet she hesitated, because it would make her dependent on one major source of credit, and although her order book was full, she knew that one of her main customers – who was also a good friend – was going through difficult times and was vague about the long-term future.

○ Cindy lit a lavender-scented purple spiral candle for wisdom, and as she slowly inhaled the gentle light her thoughts began to slow down, and the fragrance carried her to the billowing lavender bushes of her childhood garden and the distant buzz of the motorway became the honey bees.

○ As she drifted in the golden glow, she heard quite clearly the words:

Be not sad, be as the sun at midday.

The candle flame became a golden sun, high above purple mountains.

○ As Cindy came back into full consciousness, she was aware that her anxieties had receded and she was filled with confidence. The words, she recalled, came from a translation of the *I Ching*, coincidentally given to her by the friend about whom she was worried.

When she checked, the words were in the comments on the hexagram Feng (abundance, fullness) of the summer solstice, which said you should seize an opportunity and not demand guarantees. Cindy decided to go ahead with the loan, and three months later the fortunes of her main customer took an upturn and he signed an improved contract with her for two more years, thus securing her own business.

From where do the words and images come? Some say from our own deep unconscious knowledge that has assessed factors which are blocked by anxiety – in Cindy's case, an instinctive awareness that her friend was a survivor and intrinsically trustworthy. Others believe that we have access to a collective well of universal wisdom.

However, by far the majority of meditative experiences do not have such a specific outcome – yet these times of quietness and stillness are in themselves of the highest value in making contact with the spiritual world and our own higher nature.

CHAPTER TWELVE

Candles and Astral Projection

I, for one, would not like to share the belief of those who say that when the flame dies, nothing is left, that we are snuffed out like Macbeth's brief candle. Years of hearing stories from people who have had contact with loved ones from the other side have convinced me that the flame does flicker in another world, albeit one that is hidden from our eyes.

Another proof for me of the independence of the soul from the body is the amount of evidence for what are called 'out-of-body experiences', where we have the sensation of flying or floating beyond the confines of our physical form. This is almost like that conjuring trick where the magician picks the flame from a candle and carries it about in his fingers before returning it to the candle – except that in the case of 'astral projection' the meaning goes far beyond the illusion.

It is estimated that more than one-third of people in the western world have had at least one out-of-body experience. Family and friends may report that they dreamed vividly of us or even thought they saw us at a time when we were miles away in the physical body, but travelling astrally. During such experiences, we may notice that the home of the person we visited has a distinctive picture or ornament and later discover this was acquired recently without our knowledge.

Other out-of-body experiences involve feeling ourselves rising above our body and seeing it sleeping or resting below. This can occur in times of illness, stress or relaxation, or is sometimes triggered by a sudden noise.

Out-of-body experiences are usually spontaneous, but you can, with practice, learn to control the floating sensation and even to evoke an astral journey as your psychic awareness evolves.

Candles are a particularly evocative medium for experiencing astral states. During meditation with candles especially, people report the sensation of floating out of their bodies spontaneously and visiting not only friends or family, but other places and times or different dimensions. These otherworldly realms can seem almost like the sky and underworlds described by shamans or magic men and women throughout the world on their psychic journeyings.

How out-of-body experiences occur

If the mind/soul is a separate entity to the brain, then it can exist independently. Evidence from the study of near-death experiences throughout the world would suggest that people can indeed exist independently of the physical body. This astral self can then be regarded as a separate etheric or spirit body, a concept that has been suggested in both eastern and western philosophy (some say it is this etheric body that manifests as a ghost after death). Others believe that our mind has the ability to see beyond the confines of the body and out of range of normal vision, which is one interpretation of the phenomenon of remote viewing, whereby psychics describe events that may be occurring at a specific moment many miles distant.

Far from being an occult or dangerous practice, out-of-body experiences do have a deep religious and spiritual significance, and these otherworldly wanderings are self-limiting – you find that, as with meditation, the conscious world intrudes or you fall asleep when the psyche is ready to return. In Chapter 7, I have included suggestions for casting protection around yourself; if you undertake astral projection only with positive intent and when you are feeling calm and not angry or exhausted, your experiences will be fulfilling and enriching.

These soul journeys are a way of reaching every level of the mind and what the psychologist Carl Jung called the 'collective unconscious', offering access to the knowledge of all times and places, *if* we can overcome conscious barriers. So your out-of-body journeys – whether to see a friend across the other side of town or to explore the rich mythology of sky, earth and sea – are rooted in a very ancient tradition and a common spiritual need of people everywhere to explore the rich potential of the human condition.

How to undergo **an out-of-body experience**

Dusk is a good time for astral exploration (as for so much candle magic), or the early morning when it is still dark and you are totally relaxed, in that half-state between sleep and waking. The morning light flooding in will then greet you as you return from your psychic journey.

Floating out of the body
Before you begin, spend a few moments letting the darkness enfold you, as you sit or lie on a bed or soft cushions on the floor.

- Light a large single candle high in a corner of the room, placed in its holder on a fireproof tray – perhaps on top of a wardrobe or in a wall-bracket candle holder (available from household stores). The candle need not be at the top of the wall, but should be several feet above you, in the opposite corner.
- Silver, purple or deep blue are good candle colours for evoking astral travel, as are the fragrances of cinnamon, frankincense, jasmine and sandalwood, so you may wish to use a scented candle or light incense of these scents before you begin your work (see Chapter 5).
- Lie looking with half-closed eyes to the point of light, blinking if you feel the need. Play soft music or recordings of the sounds of a rainforest, flowing river or the sea to carry you gently out of your body.
- Relax your body using gentle breathing (see Chapter 11), inhaling the golden light and exhaling any negativity, so that the candlelight is gradually drawn around you as you move upwards towards it.
- Continue to draw yourself upwards diagonally to the point of light, so that you are in a vertical position with your hands outstretched. Move closer and closer, until you are enclosed within a golden sphere of light high up. Some

Images in meditation may appear within or beyond the candle flame.

people follow a tunnel or cone of light emanating from the candle and float within it until they reach the source of light.

- If you find it difficult to begin, *imagine* yourself rising and go through the whole experience like this on two or three occasions. The psychic begins where the imagination ends and the border is very blurred – you can kick-start an experience like this. Indeed, the imagination and psyche share the same channels – some practitioners call it visualization – and after a while you will find that your imaginary soul experiences are themselves incredibly rich and spiritual.
- Only if you wish, look down on your sleeping body. Float slowly and horizontally across the room, not attempting to leave it on this first occasion. When you are ready, begin to move away from the light, descending gently vertically, still with your arms outstretched.
- Many people believe that we enter and leave our bodies through the crown of our heads, known in the eastern tradition as the crown *chakra* or psychic energy centre. You may see a golden light from your head that embraces you, and you return to your body gently with a slight bump. Alternatively, you may experience a moment of mistiness, before re-entering as the etheric and physical bodies blend.
- You may find that the experience will end quite spontaneously, but if you want to return to your body, count down slowly from 100, and on the number 5 re-enter your body.

- Leave the candle to burn out if it is in a safe place or blow out the light, sending loving thoughts into the cosmos to add to positive energies.

Travelling on a pre-ordained route

- First decide where you wish to travel astrally. Choose a familiar route, perhaps to the house of a friend or relation: initially, emotional ties are a powerful incentive for out-of-body journeys.
- A day or so before trying your astral journey, travel the route in actuality, concentrating on a dozen salient landmarks and taking photographs or making careful notes, so that you can identify fine details – the grain on a front door, perhaps, or patterns on a distinctive water feature *en route*. Incorporate all your senses into this experience, so that your projected travel will rely not just on the visual sense but also on fragrances, sounds, touch and even taste.
- Practise recreating your journey in your mind two or three times when you are alone and still, and each time add more sensory detail. As a result, you may find that you experience a spontaneous out-of-body occurrence.
- If not, choose a time when it is still dark. Lie on your bed or a pile of cushions for a few moments in the darkness. Light your candle and, as before, place it in a corner high up.
- Rise slowly from your body, inhaling the light and exhaling darkness, following either a golden tunnel emanating from the candle or drawing the circle of light around you as you move diagonally upwards. You may sense a slight rush of air as you move along this path.
- Again, move horizontally, but this time leave the room, departing and returning by conventional means where possible, such as an open door or a staircase; if you do need to pass through an obstruction, such as a closed door or wall, allow it to melt to let you through, closing afterwards. You may at first sense slight resistance in a solid surface, in which case create in your mind's vision a bead curtain through which you can pass more easily.
- At first you may find that it takes as long to travel astrally as it would physically. On this first journey, travel only to the first landmark, before retracing your steps to the bed or cushions and if possible leaving the candle to burn its course.
- Gradually increase the number of landmarks you pass, moving more swiftly over the route, until you reach the chosen front door. At this stage, do not enter. Do not be surprised if people mention seeing you at the time you were journeying astrally – it is quite common for etheric doubles to be seen while on walkabout.
- When you are ready to visit your chosen destination, forewarn the friend or relation of your experiment. Generally, it is important to keep to normal visiting rules and not go into someone else's home without permission, or into private areas. Ask the host or hostess to note any particular time when your presence was sensed.
- If the person is present, greet them or gently touch a hand or shoulder. Move around the room, looking for any new features since you last visited. When you

leave, say goodbye and retrace your route – in time, you will learn to fast-forward your return journey.

○ Rest for a while afterwards, and then make a note of any important features of the experience.

Crossing the threshold: entering the light

Floating upwards and leaving the body is called etheric projection. The more visionary states, believed to occur naturally during sleep or meditation as well as being deliberately induced, are known as astral projection by purists, although most people use the terms interchangeably as I have done, because the two states have considerable overlap.

For the strictly astral form of out-of-body experience, a large, round silver or gold candle is very effective, or choose a beautiful rainbow candle shaped like a globe where the colours intermingle. A two- or three-tone candle in blues and purples will serve as well. This time the candle can be directly in line with your vision, although again in a safe place where it cannot be knocked over or burn you if you fall asleep.

True astral projection, which you have probably already experienced in dreams, can be carried out at any time during the hours of darkness, but midnight – like dusk, a threshold hour, and sometimes called the 'witching hour' because of its association with magic – is a very potent time for visionary states. The time of the full moon is especially good, and if it is warm and you have a sheltered garden, it is liberating if you can work outdoors.

○ Breathe in gently and exhale, with each inhaled breath once more drawing the focus around you so that gradually you enter it. This time, however, focus on a point within the candle as you enclose yourself in the sphere of light, and see this as a doorway or curtain of light gradually opening to allow you to pass beyond the light into another dimension. You may experience a slight sensation as you pass through the doorway of light. If you cannot, let your imagination guide you through.

○ There may be misty light on the other side of the door, but pass through and you will find yourself floating or flying through the air, swimming effortlessly through water or travelling down through tunnels into the earth, like the Christmas grottoes we visited in department stores as children. Waiting will be a guide, who will lead you and care for you as you move through these magical realms, and will take you back to the light when it is time to return.

THE ASTRAL WORLDS: A SHAMANIC JOURNEY

As mentioned earlier, shamans or magic men are the magician-priest-healers in communities in areas as far apart as India, Australia, Japan and China, Siberia and Mongolia, Africa, among the Bedouins in the Middle East and in North, Central and South America. They regularly visit the otherworldly realms to intervene on behalf of their tribes with the Mistress of Reindeer or Master of the Hunt or Sedna the Sea Mother to release shoals of fish or seals. Though we think mainly of drumming and dancing to induce these otherworldly states, shamans would

Andrew's astral **candle experience**

Andrew had two jobs, one as a magazine production editor and one in the evenings and weekends designing and making silver jewellery. But he was becoming increasingly exhausted, and his relationship with his partner Antonia was suffering because he was always busy.

After he had suffered a series of minor but debilitating illnesses, Andrew realized that he had to choose between his careers: the one in journalism, which was secure but which was filled with stress and gave him little chance for creativity, and the other in jewellery-making, which gave him great satisfaction but was far from bringing in a full-time salary.

○ Andrew lit a huge silver candle shaped like an orb, and as he looked into the flame identified an archway through which he could already see mist. He created in his imagination the moment of moving through the arch and was convinced that he would find a crossroads with two very different routes beyond it.

○ However, the first thing Andrew did see as the mist cleared was a very large red squirrel sitting on a barred gate, beyond which was a wide field of corn, scarlet in the setting sun. In the corn was Andrew's partner striding away, trampling down the ears as she walked, leaving a blackened path, as though it had been burned. The squirrel greeted Andrew and said that it would guide him, but when Andrew tried to follow his partner the corn became sharp thistles and brambles and the squirrel warned:

When the corn is cut down, the sacrifice is made and none may reverse the seasons or call the sun back from his course.

○ The squirrel darted ahead in the opposite direction, along a road that seemed to spring from nowhere, paved with silver stones and with tall silver flowers on either side. In the darkening sky glistened an enormous silver moon, much like a pendant that Andrew had recently sold.

Answering the unspoken question, the squirrel said:

You have created this road, the Beauty Way the Native Americans call it, your destined path through life. The old way is overgrown with thistle, gone from your sight.

○ Ahead was a river, but it had dried up, and on its bank was a small workshop with a gleaming workbench, engraving tools and metals of all kinds, some being smelted in a furnace. Andrew set to work and was filled with a joy he had never known as the metal formed beneath his fingers into fabulous designs, etching on the strange symbols that seemed to form into poetry in his mind. He could smell rich incense and hear chanting, and was aware that he was making offerings for a great sacrifice to Diana, goddess of the moon.

○ Tired, Andrew paused for a rest, gazing into the smelting flame that was encased in glowing copper, and suddenly the roof

sometimes retreat to a dark cave or their tents with only a single lamp to guide their psyches quietly into other dimensions.

The lower world is sometimes called the world of myth and fairytale. It can be beneath the sea or under the ground, accessed through a hole in the earth, a mineshaft or a well, or via a tree or a doorway. These visits to the underworld should not be undertaken as a form of astral tourism but are for obtaining practical help, guidance and sometimes a confrontation and mastery over our fears. Here, action is often in the form of an adventure, aided by helpful animals or mythological or archetypal figures.

The upper world is that of spirit guides, guardian angels and wise ancestors, whose fires are seen as the aurora borealis or northern lights dancing in the sky. The colours here are softer than on earth. Here reside the ancient sun and moon deities. This world can be reached by climbing a tree, ascending a rope and finding a hole in the sky or, most frequently, by flight on the back of a bird. Or you may visit earthly realms in other ages – sacred stone circles, ancient temples and opened and the silver moon seemed to plunge down to earth to meet him, filling the room as he cried:

Great goddess, take my talents in my service, take my offerings on this your day, for I worship not the sun but the moon, not gold but silver.

○ Andrew experienced wind rushing in his ears and was back, gazing at his silver candle.

What did it all mean? Andrew had tapped into ancient mythology on one level, and on another had explored his own dreamscape.

The squirrel represented an emissary in Norse mythology, which in that tradition carried messages – and insults – from the dragon at the bottom of the 'cosmic tree' to the eagle at the top, thus spanning the dimensions. Red squirrels were the special messengers of the Celtic thunder god Donar.

But what message did the squirrel bring for Andrew? That the way forward was through his silver work. Silver is the metal of the moon and of all the lunar goddesses, of dreams and intuition, and Andrew knew that a whole part of himself needed to be explored through the craft he loved.

But what of Andrew's partner? The corn field and the setting sun were symbolic of the old Celtic festival of Lughnassadh at the end of July/beginning of August – Lammas in the Christian tradition (see Chapter 9). The corn god was cut down in the last sheaf to be harvested as a sacrifice so that the crops would grow again: this death/rebirth cycle marked an ending that was necessary for a beginning.

If Andrew moved to a smaller house and cut his expenditure, he could for a time abandon the sun's way, worldly success and making money, and explore his talents. It had been Antonia's fierce opposition to a cut in income, although they were by no means impoverished, that had held Andrew in a job he no longer enjoyed but which was very well paid. Antonia had even threatened to leave if Andrew gave up his job. For some time Andrew had suspected that Antonia was being unfaithful with a new wealthy, ambitious colleague at the advertising agency where she worked. Now Andrew was forced to acknowledge with sorrow that the relationship had run its course.

He resigned from his job in journalism and moved back to his parents' home for a few months while he sorted out his finances and future alone. In the interim, he was offered the chance to rent a cheap workshop in a gallery complex, in return for giving demonstrations to tourists; he called his new business Mooncraft. Andrew is not making a fortune, but for the first time in years is deeply fulfilled.

Though Andrew had not consciously been aware of the symbolism in his astral experience, he understood the meanings of the symbols in relation to his own life.

I am convinced that we do have access to the mythology of all times and places through the collective wisdom that, as Jung suggested, lies beneath our personal unconscious. When we come across a symbol, whether from childhood fairytales or from literature, drama or art, we recall its significance and so it is very difficult to isolate the source of our knowledge. The candle flame is one route to reaching the tribal memory we all possess.

healing wells. We can all access these symbolic realms, and once you have travelled through the door you can begin to create your own scene, guided by your unconscious psyche. Whether you meet your spirit guide or a talking animal, you will pass through lands rich in myth and there derive answers to all your unspoken questions.

Your guide will take you back towards the light, although it may be by a different route, and with a gentle bump you will be back in the candle flame. Gradually the light will recede, leaving you looking once more into your candle, still and refreshed.

Let your candle burn out naturally.

CHAPTER THIRTEEN

Candles and Divination

Candles have long played a part in divination rituals. For example, there was the old country Hallowe'en custom of carrying a candle along a sheltered path from 11 o'clock until midnight, the witching hour, then taking it around the houses, farms and barns in a village. If the candle went out, it was a bad omen for the house where it extinguished, but otherwise it promised safety from witches to the houses and farms. Sometimes the candle was put in a Jack o'Lantern.

Another custom was the 'watching of the farthing candle' on St Mark's Eve, 24 April. This did not really involve a candle but a stolen pig's tail, which was set on fire. A group of young men or women would gather around it and when the tail turned blue, try to see the image of their future husband or wife in the flame.

Candle scrying

Candle scrying – gazing into a candle flame to see images – is one of the most natural forms of divination. As mentioned earlier, spontaneous candle scrying was practised in the everyday world by all who sat by candlelight, especially if they kept long vigils – for example, mothers who spent long nights gazing into the candle flame by the bedside of a sick or restless child. In the modern world, dining by candlelight creates a mood of deep relaxation where conscious barriers fade and truths are more easily spoken.

Seeing pictures in candles depends almost entirely on the visual part of our brain, which children routinely use in thinking and which we call into play when reading tealeaves or Tarot cards, or interpreting pictures in the clouds or the embers of a fire.

Symbols, our visual vocabulary, are a direct way of reaching more profound levels of experience and transcending the boundaries of time and space. They do not have the limitations of words, in which adults largely express and interpret thoughts and feelings. We do not need to be taught techniques of scrying, for we have inherited this mode of interpretation from our ancestors who lived by candlelight, although we may have forgotten or never consciously developed this method of accessing the cosmic image bank. Nor do we need a list of symbol meanings to interpret what a butterfly, a cloud or an angel means to each one of us – we have seen these images in dreams, and drawn them as children, and so they are imbued with personal significance as well as having universal meanings.

Contacting spirit guides

Many of us sense that we are protected, whether by a guardian angel, a spirit guide or our own evolved higher self. This guide may be a figure that we have dreamed of many times or an archetypal wise figure to whom we are drawn in history or literature. I have been told many times by different mediums that I have close to me a Quaker woman dressed in brown and a gypsy, figures that represent two aspects of my personality. But for some people, their guardian angel, although sensed, remains elusive. Gazing into a candle flame can evoke an image of the earthly form of this guardian.

○ Light a dark blue or purple candle whenever you feel the need to talk to your guide or receive advice, whether you believe such counsel comes from the tribal voice or collective wisdom of all mankind or from a higher being.

○ Make a special candle time in a quiet, dark room, perhaps late at night or early in the morning, and burn a fragrant incense such as frankincense or myrrh that evokes spiritual awareness and brings healing. Alternatively, use a fragrant candle as your focus.

○ Unlike in meditation, where your mind and psyche roam free, look into the flame, letting your eyes half-close, and silently ask your guardian to appear. You may find it helpful to use a glass candlestick that partially encloses the candle, so that the flame casts reflections on the glass.

○ You may see your guardian either in or beyond the candle flame or in your mind's eye, evoked by the candlelight. If you find it difficult to identify a specific figure, concentrate on the lower part of the flame close to the candle and from this build upwards and outwards – first an outline, and then fill in the details. Let a story unfold naturally about your special guide and listen to any message, which may be a single word, a phrase or part of a song.

○ If you make a regular time for candle scrying, two or three times a week or whenever you seek reassurance or wisdom, you may find that the same guide appears or there may be others, according to your mood and need. Keep a journal of any such encounters, and you may find that the messages you hear in your mind become more complex and may relate to wider issues.

○ When your guardian fades, blow out the candle and send the light and love to all who need it, not forgetting yourself.

Scrying with floating candles

Floating candles have become incredibly popular over the last three or four years and, because the flames move across the water, are a powerful form of scrying.

○ Choose richly coloured floating candles and place them in a glass bowl half-filled with water, with either crystals or glass nuggets of a lighter hue in the bottom.

○ Ask a specific question, or focus on an issue that is of importance.

○ Place the candles in a circle and light them in a clockwise formation, allowing them to move slowly across the water. Turn off the lights. If the candles are not moving, revolve the bowl nine times clockwise gently in between each image.

○ Because the light patterns are constantly changing, you may get four or five images, from the water between the candles or from the pattern of the flames as they touch and move apart. Note these, and let them form a story in your mind as you watch the candles gently moving.

○ Leave the candles to burn down. As they burn through, you may find that wax breaks away and leaves an image on the water. Read this too.

Light falls on water in ever-changing images, unfolding the story of future paths.

○ You can also use floating candles on water in a dark bowl, or with water coloured black with inks or a dark infusion such as mugwort, or any dark liquid such as black tea or coffee.

Scrying with candles, crystals and mirrors

In ancient Greece, young boys were used for scrying. They were told to gaze into bowls of pure water lit by burning torches. They studied the changes in the water in the flickering light and invoked the gods or demons to provide meaning. Though we no longer believe in summoning spirits, or the *divus* or god (from which the word divination is derived), we can, by gazing into a crystal ball, a large crystal, a small pool, a bowl of water or a mirror on which flickering candlelight falls, access wisdom to answer questions or give insight.

Sue's floating candle divination

Sue is in her forties and a book editor. She is married with a teenage son, but has recently started an affair which she says has improved the quality of her marriage because she herself is happier. However, she worries about the future and feels guilty about deceiving her husband.

○ The first patterns of light Sue sees on the water suggest a knight in shining armour galloping into the distance, which she identifies as her romantic younger lover, who has swept her off her feet and makes her feel young and vibrant. However, he has shown no signs of wanting to commit himself to Sue in a permanent relationship and has, she acknowledges for the first time, a roving eye.

○ The second symbol is a hermit, which she identifies as her husband, who has become increasingly remote over the years but whom she feels, ironically, she has moved closer to with her own new zest for life. Both of these are Tarot images, a form of divination she does not use, and so the symbols may have emerged from the source of archetypal imagery to which we all have access, or her own personal mythological store gained through reading.

○ The third symbol is a knotted rope that Sue sees as tying her, but which she senses she can undo if she makes a decision, rather than letting life sweep her along.

What is the rope? Sue admits she feels trapped as well as excited by her lover, who demands that she sees him whenever he asks but who does not want forevers. She also says that in spite of her apparent willingness to sacrifice all for love, she does fear losing her marriage and home if she is discovered, as she knows her son would not approve of her dalliance.

○ The next symbol is an hour glass, in which she sees the sand has almost run through. Initially, Sue insists that this is her life passing and that she must seize happiness before it fades. But then she wonders if it means that time is running out for her double life and she must choose. Both meanings are valid and do not exclude each other.

○ As the candles burn down, a piece of wax breaks off, which she forms into a heart that then splits in two. Sue says that she knows that she must give up her lover in the near future, as ultimately the guilt and fear will outweigh the joy. Can she rekindle her faded love for her husband?

○ The final symbol that forms in the water is a steep hill with a distant figure, the hermit again, waiting at the top of a stony track. It will be an uphill struggle, but one she accepts she must try.

○ Each symbol has acted as a focus and trigger for recognizing feelings that Sue has denied, offering a clearer if not desirable course of future action – all scrying and divination can only point to possible ways forward. Maybe Sue will end up alone, or perhaps with a more meaningful relationship with her husband.

Sue did not act after the divination, but after she was seen by a neighbour in the local town with her lover, she realizes that time is perhaps running out.

○ Deep blue, purple or silver are traditional scrying colours, as is white. Place candles in all four corners of the room, and one or two just out of your direct line of vision but which shine into the reflective surface, so that you have a central pool of light and more distant, diffused beams. The candles should be higher than the scrying medium. You may wish to open a window slightly so that the candles flicker.

○ Alternatively, place a semi-circle of five small candles on the far side of the crystal. Five is a traditional number of candles for scrying, but experiment with different numbers, sizes and shapes.

○ You can scry using either clear water, a mirror, a crystal or a darkened sphere, or dark water. Experiment to find which works for you.

○ For all candle scrying, keep a notebook close by so that you can record any impressions.

Scrying with light

Just before dawn is a good time for scrying in clear surfaces. Use a clear crystal such as quartz, a crystal ball or a sphere such as a paperweight, or even a brandy glass.

○ Fill a clear glass or crystal bowl with pure water: either mineral water from a former sacred spring or rainwater that has not touched anything – such as a roof or gutter – as it fell to the ground. You can leave the bowl outside to collect the rain. Modern indoor water features or small fountains with a bowl are ideal for scrying by candlelight.

○ Alternatively, keep a medium-sized oval mirror especially for scrying and wrap it in dark silk when not in use.

○ Think of a question or issue as you light your candles and extinguish any other lights. Allow the ideas to flow freely rather than trying to force them in one direction or another.

○ Sit on one side of the bowl or crystal and cup your hands around it.

○ Alternatively, if you are using a crystal or a crystal or agate egg, hold the crystal or egg in your left hand and turn it slowly clockwise from the top nine times. As you do so, repeat your question or recite your need nine times. Hold the egg or crystal up to the light between your hands and you will see pictures of light and shadow unfolding on the surface. These may be scenes of your own life or symbols that point a way forward. Finally, turn your egg again, this time anti-clockwise nine times, and as you do this the answer to your question will come into your head.

○ If you are mirror scrying, place your seat slightly to the right, at an angle of about 45 degrees, so that you cannot see your own reflection in the mirror and the picture is slightly out of focus. Experiment with candles around the sides and in front of the mirror – you may need more candles than for water or crystal scrying, so that their reflections fall in different areas of the glass.

○ With all these media, gaze into the surface and let impressions come which may be images in the water or in your mind's vision, colours, pictures, sounds, even fragrances. Although candle scrying does primarily evoke visual or clairvoyant (literally 'clear seeing') responses, once you have awakened your psychic senses you may experience clairaudience (sounds not from the external world), psychometric impressions through your fingertips, and clairsentience (impressions and scents, spices or homely smells such as baking bread) – see also Chapter 14.

○ If nothing appears, close your eyes, open them and blink, then look into the water. You may see whole pictures or sense images, rather than actually seeing single images when you scry.

○ Do not try to analyse your results, but record them, using pictures if this is easier. Read them after you have extinguished the candles, and if answers do not instantly emerge they will do so as you go about your day. Some people see these images primarily in their mind's eye – this is just as valid.

Scrying with shadows

Shadow scrying is best done at dusk or during the evening before midnight. A blue beryl or polished amethyst or rose quartz crystal will reflect candlelight, and you can see images in the contrast between light and shadow. Obsidian, a dark black crystal through which light shines, is a very ancient device for shadow scrying. A dark, smoked curved glass serves a similar purpose. Agates have been used for many centuries in Asia for scrying.

Opaque agate, onyx and marble eggs, especially those of green and yellow, are excellent for shadow scrying and can be bought very cheaply. You do not need a large sphere. Buy one that you can hold comfortably in your hands so you can turn it to catch the reflections of candlelight and shadow on its surface.

Mirrors of highly polished metal were consulted in ancient China to study what would come to pass. The Greeks also scryed in bronze mirrors to see into the future. Black shiny mirrors, often called witches' mirrors, were popular in medieval times, but because of their association with darker practices are now rarely possessed by ordinary scryers.

For a traditional witches' black mirror, you can substitute a large black-glossed tile, or use a silver, brass, copper or stainless steel tray. Again, keep this exclusively for scrying, covered with a dark cloth when not in use, and polish it before each reading. For water scrying, use a metallic or dark glass or cookware bowl and tint the water with inks, herbal infusions or even black tea or coffee. One woman I know is able to scry successfully with cola!

The combination of fire and water provides a rippling, shimmering light that forms a curtain made of beads of light, which will part to reveal the words that you can see either in your mind's eye or in the reflective surface, or hear as words in your ear.

○ Use a large bowl of dark water and place five white candles on the other side from you, a short distance away so that you can see their light on the water.

○ Ripple the water nine times anti-clockwise with a hazel, ash or rowan twig – all woods of divination – or with a clear white crystal, and use the whirling lights to pass through the curtain.

○ Visualize in the water a temple in the clearing of a wood, with a large jewelled book raised high in the entrance.

Jordan's candle scrying

Jordan was a successful businessman but felt something was missing from his life. He said that he had worked from leaving school, but at 50 he was aware that relationships and his spiritual side had always been relegated to second place.

On holiday in Italy, he had met an American woman who owned a bar and restaurant and they had enjoyed a brief but passionate affair. He had promised to return and she had now written suggesting he come back to Italy for a month or two in the quiet season so that they could spend time together. Jordan felt that he could not leave his business for so long, although he had competent managers, but since the holiday he had found it almost impossible to settle back into his life.

Sceptical of all matters psychic, Jordan was persuaded to try this technique by his sister, who assured him he could use it psychologically, rather like the ink-blot test. Some people argue that divination is no more than a way of exploring existing options – even on that level it is a valuable tool for bringing unconsidered factors to light – but many see these processes as far more profound and spiritual.

- Jordan stirred the water self-consciously, and to his own surprise said he could see a very small dark hut among tangled branches, and a dusty book.
- When he swirled the water for a second time, he heard words that were his and yet, he said, they sounded as if they belonged to someone much older:

There can be no gain without loss, and whether we follow the road or sit by the wayside watching the travellers, we carry what we are always within. To journey may lead us back home, but we can only know if we venture forth, following our own light.

No promises of eternal happiness for Jordan, only self-knowledge. He did go for a month to Italy, but realized that his love affair was just a holiday romance. However, when he came back, he decided to make major changes and went on several courses to increase his spiritual awareness, on one of which he met his future partner.

- Swirl the water nine times, this time clockwise, and as the water slows you will see words or pictures in the candlelight, either in your mind's eye or on the surface, or hear words spoken from some distant source that are relevant to your present situation and a guide to future choices.
- Leave the bowl and candles to burn down in a safe place.

Wax *divination*

This is one of the earliest forms of divination and can be practised either separately or after another form of candle scrying.

- Light a white candle and sit in the darkness looking into the flame, but without focusing on any special matters. If you see images in the flame, note what they are.
- When you feel ready, drip white wax on to a thick piece of dark paper, while asking a question or focusing on an issue in your life, and continue to do so until you have an image. This will relate to the current concern.

Wax divination in water

In another method, wax or molten lead would be thrown into a bucket of cold water to make a picture. This is especially potent outdoors after dark and was traditionally practised on New Year's Eve to identify a potential lover.

- Use a heatproof pottery or glass bowl filled with clear water. Ring your bowl with vibrantly coloured candles – for example, red, dark blue, purple, gold or green – as the method does not work so well with pastel colours.
- Tip a single candle colour on the surface of the water while thinking of a question or issue that concerns you.
- You need to be very quick in order to interpret your first image before the wax hardens. This first image shows you hidden aspects of the present situation or any opposition you are facing. Usually it is a single image.
- As the wax hardens, you will have a second static picture – an initial or a shape – that you can study at length. This will suggest a solution.

Wax divination using several candles

A third method of wax divination involves using several small, thick candles placed directly on to a metal tray or dish in a circle, so that the melting wax can flow freely. Make sure that the surface is flat. Use dark or bold, contrasting colours and watch as the colours merge to make pictures.

- Alternatively, if you are in a work or emotional situation where several people are involved, designate a candle for each one. Scratch the name of the person lightly in the wax.
- Light the candles and watch how the colours interact and which candle wax flows into other candles. Two furthest away may join. See which is consumed first and which burns longest.

Wax divination offers solutions to modern dilemmas, as it once guided our ancestors in their questionings.

Linda's candle **relationships**

Linda was the co-ordinator of a design team and she had been experiencing trouble with two senior female members, Susan and Cynthia, who seemed to be undermining all her decisions. Geoff, her deputy, told Linda to ignore the problem as it was not really as bad as it seemed. He offered to have a word with the women, but suggested that Linda should ease off her own workload, as she was obviously under stress that might be contributing to her overreaction.

- Linda lit a blue candle for herself, green for Geoff the peacemaker, yellow for Cynthia, who was always making spiteful remarks, and red for Susan, who was perpetually angry.
- Her own candle burned slowly, but Geoff's candle began to shed wax almost at once, although all the candles were of the same make and kind. His wax actually moved behind Linda's candle and split in two, half flowing to Cynthia's and half to Susan's. As it reached their candles, their wax flowed in straight lines towards Linda, but stopped short.
- Geoff's wax seemed to be fuelling the yellow and red candles and all three flowed to surround Linda. This was totally unexpected. Was Geoff the peacemaker actually behind the hostility of the other two women towards Linda? It seemed unlikely, but Linda took the opportunity to talk separately and non-confrontationally to Susan and Cynthia. Geoff, it seemed, had been spreading rumours that Linda intended to sack the two women and replace them with friends of hers; this was totally untrue. Susan and Cynthia admitted they had responded to the rumour with open hostility towards Linda.

What was in it for Geoff? To drive Linda out, to take her job but not, as he had promised the other two, to split the deputy's post between them. Linda discovered from a chat with Geoff's girlfriend Annie, a junior with a similar firm, that he had also promised to bring in Annie as senior.

Once Linda, Susan and Cynthia united, Geoff realized that his own position was untenable and he moved on. The signs were there, but it took the candles to bring them to Linda's notice.

- You may find some surprising correlations with the people concerned and some unexpected liaisons that interact. You can learn a great deal about the hidden group dynamics by observing, for example, which colour is swamped by the other candles, which moves away and which allies (merges) with another. I have found this one of the most powerful ways of revealing underlying trends I had entirely missed on a conscious level.

Candle **options**

If you have two options, light two candles of identical size, colour and length in matching candlesticks and place them side by side in a draughtproof spot.

- Under each candlestick, put a piece of paper on which you have named the option or person that each candle represents.
- As you light each candle, endow the flame with all your hopes and fears.
- The candle to remain alight longest represents the correct choice. Sometimes one may go out very quickly, and this is often the path or person preferred consciously that may offer instant results or excitement, but in the longer perspective will not endure. If both candles go out almost instantaneously, now is not the time to ask, so try another day.
- Leave the candle of the wise choice to burn in a safe place.

CHAPTER FOURTEEN

Candle Magic and Past Lives

Candles can light your path back to past times. Past-life regressions have become increasingly popular in the West with the growing acceptance among some sections of the population of reincarnation – the belief that our soul returns to a new body after death. It has long been central to Eastern religions.

In my own work, I have come across startling cases of spontaneous past-world recall. Adam, a three-year-old boy living in the north of England, showed his parents the spot where, he said, his plane had crashed. Local historians revealed that a plane had crashed in that spot during World War II in the manner described by the child. Other small children have spoken of fatal motorbike or car crashes in which they were once involved, sometimes using vocabulary that was far beyond their years. Seconds later they have no recall of the remarks and rarely can they be persuaded to repeat them.

As already mentioned, the psychologist Carl Jung believed that we have access to a universal tribal memory, the 'collective unconscious'. This would explain our recall of past lives as the act of tapping into a particular archetypal symbol with which our present situation or need is linked.

There is evidence that by using techniques such as hypnosis, visualization and meditation, it is possible to regress to past lives and gain knowledge that may be useful in the present. Some people may be worried about being regressed hypnotically, and you do have to be careful in the choice of a therapist.

However, a flickering candle flame offers a gentle but powerful doorway to that earlier, slower world where people rose by the sun and lit candles as dusk fell. You do not need to enter a deep trance to practise past-life candle magic. Because candles and fires have formed part of an unbroken heritage of festivals and rituals in every age and almost every place, the treasurehouse of candle past-life experiences is almost inexhaustible.

The path to **the past**

You can adapt any of the methods that you practise for candle scrying (see Chapter 13) to past-life candle magic. The only difference is that instead of asking a direct question about the present or future, you focus on moving backwards.

You will need to create a pathway using candles that will direct your psychic energies towards the past rather than present or future issues, although in practice they are all entwined.

In time, your past-life experiences may occur spontaneously, either when you are scrying or simply sitting quietly by candlelight.

○ You will need three candles and a large mirror. This method is best practised in the evening when you are calm and quiet.

Reflected light offers a pathway through the mirror to the past, recalled perhaps dimly in dreams.

- In a darkened room, light three candles so that the flames form a pathway into the mirror and their reflections continue the path into the distance.
- Sit just behind the candle furthest from the mirror and slightly to the side, so that you do not see your own reflection in the glass.
- Look beyond the first flame to the second, then the third, and follow the candles into the mirror. You may experience a slight jolt or a momentary mist.
- When you reach the first light in the mirror, pause and look round in the darkness. See what shadowy forms are around you: perhaps hills, trees or buildings.
- Move on to the second light in the mirror, where the scene will be clearer. You may now hear sounds and smell fragrances. Feel grass or sand beneath your feet. There may be a figure walking beside you – perhaps your guardian, whom you met in the glass when you were scrying, or it may be someone belonging to the world you are entering who will protect and guide you. You may feel you have known the person a very long time. You can ask any questions you wish and these will be answered truthfully. Continue walking to the third and final flame in the mirror.
- This flame acts as your entry point into the past world and is a golden doorway through which you can leave at any time. Let your guardian lead the way. You may find yourself in a building, perhaps a house. You may see people, and identify someone who was once you or with whom you feel close kinship. It is like watching a play unfold. You cannot intervene, nor can you be harmed,

Cathy's **candle pathway**

Cathy was concerned that although her business, which involved organizing tours of vineyards in Europe, was thriving, she was spending much of the year away from her husband and teenage children, who were becoming strangers. Recently she had been offered a desk job with a wine merchant. It would provide a regular but much lower salary and plenty of time at home. However, she felt that she could not bear to give up her successful and fulfilling career.

- Cathy lit her candles, and as she reached the first candle was aware of vineyards at night, falling away from the roadside, lit only by a single star ahead.
- When Cathy arrived at the second candle in the mirror, she met an old woman in a cloak whose face Cathy had often seen in dreams, and she smelled an overwhelming scent of flowers after rain. The old woman said nothing, but Cathy felt that for the first time in years she was protected.
- At the third candle, Cathy entered

a huge dark castle with many rooms, most of which were shut as if the occupants had gone away. At last, in a tower she found a young woman who looked remarkably like Cathy herself in medieval dress, spinning. The woman was entirely alone, except for an old servant woman who came into the turret and threw logs on the fire, because although the sun was shining outside, the tower was dark and cold. From the window, Cathy could see that the vineyards were untended. She knew, without words being spoken, that she or the young woman had been abandoned, as her husband and all the workers had gone to the Crusades, and that life was passing her by, the crops failing and that she felt totally helpless.

I will never be in this position again.

Cathy vowed – or perhaps it was the abandoned wife who spoke.

- Cathy left the woman, and as her guardian retreated into the flame

she spoke these words to Cathy:

The vines will grow again, but love will not.

Cathy puzzled over her experience, but that night dreamed of her childhood, with her feckless but charming father and her mother who had been constantly depressed by money worries. Cathy realized that her determination to be both financially independent and also successful was built on the real fears of her childhood, and the feelings of helplessness and being abandoned from her past world had taken her away from her family, for whom she was working. Whether this was an actual experience or a symbolic one, it helped Cathy to recognize and face the deep-seated twin fears of abandonment and lack of control over her destiny that drove her.

Cathy did not take the desk job, but has taken on assistant so that now she herself travels much less. Although the family have less money, Cathy is beginning to discover herself as a wife and mother again, before it was too late.

for these are living memories. Follow the person with whom you identify or ask your guardian to show you whatever it is you need to know. After a while the voices will become fainter and the light more dim and you should make your way back to the golden doorway.

- Move now directly towards the second candle and the mirror ahead. There is no hurry, but when you reach the second flame thank your guardian or guide and leave him or her at the candle reflection, which may now have become a watchtower.
- Move back to the third candle, the one nearest the mirror. Perhaps now you will understand the significance of the shadowy scenes you witnessed on your way inwards.
- Focus on the first candle on the other side of the mirror and you may again experience a slight jolt as you pass through the mirror. Continue until you are sitting behind the first candle again.

- Sit quietly in the candlelight, letting the impressions flow over you. You may be surprised at how little time has passed, because time in other dimensions is very different.
- When you are ready, blow out each candle, beginning with the one nearest to you, and pause, watching its alter ego in the mirror also blank out.
- As you extinguish the second candle, you may see in the mirror a glimpse of your guardian in the afterglow and even feel a touch as light as gossamer.
- Finally, blow out the last candle and sit in the darkness with only the mirror glow, letting the pieces of the experience form coherent images in your mind.
- Try to spend the rest of the evening listening to music or watching the moon and the stars. When you go to sleep, your dreams may continue the pathways you trod.

The pathway of **fragrance**

The evocative magic of the candle can conjure up past worlds. But it may help to add fragrances associated with the past, as these can trigger the collective memory.

For past-life recall, beeswax candles are especially potent, as they can trace a path back to the Mother Goddess, sometimes called the Bee Goddess. The Roman earth and corn goddess Demeter was associated with the bee and her handmaidens were called *melissae* (Latin for bees).

You might like to begin this ritual on a summer evening when bees are flying around. If possible, you should make your own beeswax candles. Use natural yellow undyed beeswax. As you roll out the shape, let the gentle honeyed fragrance carry you in your mind's eye to hives of long ago set in an orchard. If you are unable to make the candles, you may be able to buy them in the shape of a flower or bee.

Carry out the ritual in a place of calm where there are no unnecessarily distracting artificial sounds, such as washing machines and radios, immediately around you. An ideal place is a garden.

- Decorate the base of your candle holder with fragrant yellow flowers. Sip a nectar drink or herbal tea of summer flowers, sweetened with honey.
- As dusk falls, light a single beeswax candle with a taper or match.
- Hold a teaspoon of honey in your mouth and as you eat it, absorb slowly the honeyed fragrance of the beeswax candle.
- Slowly and deeply inhale golden yellow fragrance, then exhale slowly. Visualize that with each breath out, you are all expelling all darkness and current concerns from your body and your life. Visualize a dark mist leaving your lips and dissipating in the evening air.
- Focus on the flame and let it slowly enfold you, so that the fragrance of honey excludes all other senses. The candle flame becomes the glowing sun reflected in shimmering water and it is light again. See a hive in the orchard and in your mind's vision walk towards it, letting the sound of the bees lull you.

- A large bee flies out of the hive and you follow it wherever you need to go. A bee entering a house traditionally heralds good luck and the arrival of a stranger. You are protected, because a bee will not dwell where there is anger or malice.
- Your bee may take you anywhere, but will favour sunny places and pollen-rich flowers. You may link into candle celebrations, or the world of the candle-maker, or a country place where the bees are loud and the sun is warm. Beeswax experiences tend to be warm and reassuring.
- If you listen and observe, you may find the past person who is connected in some way to your present and perhaps your future, for bees are harbingers of future events. If the theory of circular time is correct, those whom you are visiting across the ages may be aware of you as a light breeze or a presence. You are the future of the vision you see and so it is important to tread lightly. Let the experience flow all around you.
- You will become aware of the bee hovering close to you and this is a signal that it is time to return. Follow the bee back to the hive, remembering to tell the bees of any important news in your life or perhaps insights from your experience.
- Sitting against a tree, let the brilliance of the sunshine on water become once again the candle flame and move towards it, until you are sitting in the dusk again by candlelight.
- Let the candle burn down naturally. If you look at the shapes made by the melting wax, you will identify a symbol from the past world you explored that will hold the key to the meaning of the experience.
- As with the candle and mirror regressions, after a time you may discover that even when you are using a beeswax candle for a ritual for love, money or health, a momentary vision of older worlds may appear quite unbidden and shed insight on an issue you had not even consciously acknowledged.

The pathway of **the planets**

The connection between the celestial realms and the earthly plane is one shrouded in mystery. The ancients knew the planets visible to the naked eye and gave them the names of the classical deities: for example, Mercury was named after the messenger of the gods because of the speed with which it moved through the sky, and Mars, with its red glow, was named after the god of war.

Certain fragrances have become associated with the qualities of the planets, and when these are burned as scented candles they evoke not only those strengths but past-life scenes associated with them. While the candle past-life work described earlier allows the psyche to wander freely, this more focused form of candle regression can be used to ask specific questions or to understand fears and phobias. Choose the planet most relevant to your current need (see below). As with all candle magic, you may see pictures within the flame, around it, beyond it or in your mind, recalling scenes where the fragrances once predominated.

Before you begin your planetary candle work, you should stand under the stars and, using a star map, try to identify the planets. You may see the planet whose

Candle smoke rises, offering candle visions of the sun, to inspire confidence and the ability to overcome obstacles.

energies you are calling shining quite brightly, and that is especially magical. The sun at transition times between day and night – dawn or dusk – is best for past-life candle magic, and the moon in its waning phase is most potent for looking backwards through time.

Lunar candle visions

These can be invoked for all questions concerned with the cycles of life, women, fertility, fulfilling dreams, intuition, fears of the dark, insomnia and nightmares, compulsions and addictions, and an inability to accept reality.

Jasmine is the fragrance of the moon. The folk name for jasmine is 'moonlight on the grove', and it is a fragrance associated with prophetic visions. Leave the candle burning in your bedroom before you go to bed, so that its scent can pervade your senses while you sleep; leave it in a safe place, or use a jasmine-scented night light to carry you into the world of enchantment that began with the early moon worshippers.

A trinity of huge carved stone goddesses, representing the three main cycles of the moon, was found in a cave at the Abri du Roc aux Sorciers at Angles-sur-l'Anglin in France, dating from between 13,000BC and 11,000BC. Perhaps you may visit the glades of Diana, goddess of the moon, the hunt and fertility – although, like her Greek counterpart Artemis, she was worshipped originally as the maiden aspect of the moon, in time she came to represent the full moon also. Perhaps you may find yourself working in the fields under the brilliant light of the harvest moon, which rose as the sun set, or waking as the full moon made your bedroom as bright as day. You may see jasmine growing in some exotic place, flowering in the moonlight.

- Using the candle flame as the focus, breathe in the jasmine fragrance and let it expand until you are looking upwards at a full moon in a clear, ink-black sky.
- Follow the path of the moonlight, and keep walking until you encounter a group of people and you can identify a special person who is linked to you. Listen to their words and those who interact with the person who was a part of you, either actually or symbolically.
- When you are ready to return, follow the path of the moon and the fragrance of jasmine until the moon becomes a candle.
- Close your eyes and let the scent overpower you, and you will understand your fears and so be able to begin to overcome them. You may need to visit the jasmine world again if your resolve falters, and may return to the same scene if it still has knowledge to impart to you.

Solar candle visions

These can be induced for all questions concerning confidence, success, health, energy, new beginnings, power and potential, and for illnesses due to overwork, stress or burnout, and nervous skin rashes.

Use a candle scented with frankincense, the fragrance of the sun. It was burned by the ancient Egyptians each morning at sunrise to greet the solar god Ra as he began his journey across the sky in his solar boat. The Magi offered it as a gift to the infant Christ.

Burn your frankincense candle at dawn while facing east, for visions of other sunrises promising new tomorrows, of Druids greeting the dawn of the longest day when the sun is at its height, of deserts and ancient pyramids, of orange and olive groves bathed in light and exotic spices being loaded on to wooden ships for their journeys across the world, and of rituals both pagan and Christian, where people have consigned their prayers to the rising fragrance of incense, cool marble temples and high vaulted cathedrals.

- Light your candle so that the first rays of sunlight will give it power and close your eyes, to rise upwards on the fragrance as worshippers have done over the centuries.
- Open your eyes to see candles and perhaps an incense censer or burner in another setting. Look at the wall behind the candles, or the trees if you are performing this rite in the open air, and gradually widen your focus to the celebration, service or ritual, hearing the words and the chants, and looking once more for the person with whom you can identify.
- As the ceremony ends, follow your alter ego as he or she returns home or to a place of work and let the scene unfold, especially any plans for the future or dreams that are expressed or are being pursued by the 'you' person or those around him or her.
- When you are ready to return, look for a shaft of sunlight, a candle, fire or a blazing torch that will become your candle flame.
- Extinguish your candle, sending the love to all who are making new beginnings.
- Go for an early morning walk and concentrate on the rhythm of your feet, pushing away all conscious thoughts of the everyday world. As you walk, you

will tune back into your sun candle experiences and understand their significance in your present life.

○ If you can find a pool or pond with sunlight reflected in it, the golden moving symbols may echo your insights.

Candle visions of Mercury

These should be invoked when you have questions about matters involving communication, learning, money, travel, healing, intrigue and trickery, the inability to continue a course or relationship, restlessness and hyperactivity.

Use a lavender-scented candle – the fragrance of Mercury, planet of communication – on misty or rainy mornings for visions of music, glimpses of long journeys, herbalists and wise healers, departures, laughter and crowds of people at carnivals or circuses and adventures of all kinds. Mercury was the winged messenger of the Roman gods (known as Hermes to the Greeks). Carrying his caduceus, a healing rod entwined with two serpents, he took messages between the heavens, earth and the underworld. By his skill and dexterity, he came to rule over music, commerce and medicine, and also tricksters and thieves. So this past path may be helpful if you are ill or have fallen prey to deceivers.

Although love is traditionally associated with lavender, its mercurial associations mark it as a fragrance of healing and movement (think of the wind blowing through lavender, carrying its soothing perfume far and wide).

○ Light your candle where there is a slight breeze that moves the flame without extinguishing it.

○ As you look into the moving flame, picture a field of lavender on a flat plain and a yellow butterfly hovering over it.

○ Follow the butterfly, who will guide you – but be prepared to move swiftly and for a constantly changing scene.

○ You may be led to someone whose wise actions and words can help you to heal someone close to you, or whose cunning can counteract the guile surrounding you in business dealings or relationships.

○ When the vision has passed, go for a walk in the real world to absorb the lessons of other times.

Candle visions of Venus

These visions may be helpful for questions concerning love, relationships, affairs, fidelity, families, reconciliation, betrayals in love, jealousy and passion.

Use a rose-scented candle – the fragrance of Venus, goddess of love. Venus, whose Greek name was Aphrodite (meaning 'born of the foam') was beauty incarnate, the Roman goddess of love and seduction. Her most famous offspring was Cupid (Eros to the Greeks), fathered by Mars, so uniting love and war.

As night falls, lighting this candle during the period of the new moon may bring pictures of rose gardens and young lovers, of secret trysts under cover of darkness, of promises made beneath the new moon, of passions such as that of Paris for Helen that led to war between Greek and Trojan, of weddings, births, anniversaries, homes filled with children and animals.

- Light your rose candle in a sheltered place in the garden so that you can look through the flame at a rose bush or, if indoors, at a vase of golden and red roses.
- Inhale the fragrance as pink light and exhale all negative feelings, and gradually let the flame merge in your mind's vision with the flowers, so that you are standing next to another rose bush in a different time and place, touching the soft petals and able to move beyond it.
- Tread softly in case you stumble across a secret meeting, perhaps of your alter ego and a forbidden love.

Candle visions of Mars

When you are vexed by bullying and violence, if you need courage to face change or threats to your survival or physical or mental well-being, if you are forced to defend yourself or your family, these visions can strengthen and sustain you.

Use a pine-scented candle – the cleansing fragrance of Mars, god of war and also courage – for visions of forests, mountains and scenes of nature at its most turbulent and magnificent. Mars (called Ares by the Greeks) was the father of Romulus and Remus, legendary founders of Rome. As god of both agriculture and war, Mars represented the ideal Roman, first as farmer and then as a conqueror. To his quality of courage is added a nobility of spirit when his anger and warlike nature are directed against injustice and inertia.

Your candle may summon up visions of tall trees blown by the wind or winter celebrations with pines decorated with candles, for as god of iron Mars is associated with the forge and with fire. You may witness transport of all kinds, forges and furnaces, ploughs creating fertility out of barren soil through sheer determination, battles, wartime experiences, valour and also struggles against oppressors. These are exciting and stimulating visions that will help to clear the path for change.

- Light your candle on dark afternoons by an open fire on which you have thrown pine needles, or use a large candle of the kind used at Yule, scented with pine.
- Gaze into the candle flame and see the light glinting on metal. Let the metal object come into focus, be it a weapon, the side of a plane, an anvil, a wheel on a cart or vehicle track through a pine forest, or a huge iron pot in an old kitchen. See who is holding, propelling or driving the metal: it may be your alter ego or someone close to him or her.
- If you are in the midst of a battle, find a safe hiding place from which to observe the encounter.
- You can return at any time by focusing on metal. Afterwards, go for a walk in a wood or forest if possible, where you may find a symbol of the past-life experience.

Candle visions of Jupiter

Such visions can offer help with questions concerning conscious wisdom, happiness, the acquisition of knowledge through experience, and the expansion of horizons. They may help you deal with the constraints of tradition and convention, justice and injustice, dogma and authoritarianism.

Use a sandalwood-scented candle – the fragrance of Jupiter, the sky-father, who was the supreme Roman god. Like his Greek counterpart Zeus, he controlled the thunderbolts, which were carried by his eagle, the king of the birds. He ruled not despotically but as the chief of a triumvirate of gods; before using his third avenging thunderbolt, Jupiter consulted the superior or hidden gods. In time he became regarded as the heavenly form of the earthly Roman emperor.

Sandalwood, a ceremonial fragranced wood associated with spirituality, power and protection, may evoke scenes of formal celebrations and triumphs, pageants and slow processions, courts of justice, seats of learning and royal palaces. There may also be old, wise souls to offer advice, seers, sages and scribes from many traditions.

- Light your candle when thunder rumbles in the sky or on a wild night when the heavens are in motion.
- As you look at the candle, visualize a magnificent eagle soaring upwards.
- Follow him as he soars over mountains and through the storm towards the sun, for he will take you to places of extremes and to noble courts where you can listen to the counsels of the wise and perhaps see your alter ego, and also eagerly absorb an ancient tradition whose truths can offer insight.
- Return when the eagle calls you – and he may come back for you another day.

Candle visions of Saturn

These may help when you are troubled by questions concerning spirituality, limitations and restrictions, secrecy and mystery, an acceptance of inevitable changes, inner wisdom and the acquisition of knowledge through setbacks, ageing, endings of all kinds that lead to beginnings after lessons to be learned, and issues of mortality and immortality.

Use a cypress-scented candle – the fragrance of Saturn, the planet of restriction. In mythology, Saturnus (the Roman form of Cronus, god of time) was Jupiter's father, who was deposed by his son. Saturnus therefore had to bow to the inevitable; time and progress cannot be held back and the old order must give way to the new. Saturnus was sent to Italy, where he taught the farmers agriculture and engineering and established a Golden Age of peace and plenty.

Your cypress candle may take you to ancient shrines, medicine wheels and standing stones, sites of spiritual power which have lost their earthly dominance, to mysterious rites, and to the workshops of alchemists and wizards. Because of the duality of Saturn, you may also experience small cameos of working life: tool shops, factories, schools and homes full of activities that come under his auspices as the progressor of small endeavours.

- Light your cypress candle at midnight and sit very quietly, as the candle flame becomes a lantern carried by a hermit or traveller.
- Progress will be slow down dark passages and up steep rocky paths, but if you have the patience to follow, you will understand much about your own frailties and those of your fellow man, and be liberated from their power.

PART FOUR

Formal **Candle Magic**

CHAPTER FIFTEEN

Candles and the Elements

In formal magic, the four ancient elements are seen as providing natural energies for transforming wishes into actuality. Earth, air, fire and water in this sense are not chemical elements, but symbols of the four forces that traditionally make up life on the physical, mental and spiritual planes, not only in mankind, but throughout the universe. Together, they combine to form the fifth element, ether or *akasha*, that represents pure spirit or perfection.

Candle magic is recognized as unique, in that the four elements are contained within the candle, so the fifth is created in candle magic to empower any desire. The late American psychic author Scott Cunningham pointed out that the candle itself represents the element of earth. When brought to life by the element of fire, the candle melts, producing liquid wax, the element of water, and smoke, the element of air.

However, generally four distinctive candles are used to represent the four elements, one in the centre of each of the quadrants of the circle that is used in more formal magical rituals.

Each candle provides the focus for the qualities of each element and so, whether used separately in a ritual or to balance the energies of the circle, is in itself a source of power and protection. What is more, because we are made up of these symbolic elements in differing proportions, each can offer strength in a particular area of our life and personality.

Begin by getting in touch with each of the elements in turn, at times when you need their particular qualities in your life.

Earth

Earth is the element of order, both in nature and in institutions such as the law, politics, finance, health and education. It also represents the female, yin, nurturing goddess aspect, Mother Earth, the home and the family, as well as money and security, and is a good element to invoke when a step-by-step or practical approach is needed in your life. (Yin, and its counterpart yang, are the complementary positive/negative, female/male energies in Chinese philosophy.)

If you have a large proportion of earth in your make-up, you will be kind and caring towards others, practical, persevering and cautious.

Its elemental creatures are gnomes, with their stores of hidden treasure, wisdom and, above all, common sense. You may see one fleetingly in your garden or near caves, brown and not at all like the colourful Disney gnomes. They are a reminder that what is of worth does not necessarily offer instant excitement or results.

Colours Green, brown **Quarter** North **Direction** Night **Season** Winter

Zodiacal signs Taurus, Virgo, Capricorn

○ Surround your green or brown earth candle with grains, berries, fruits, coins or pot pourri, and place it so that you face north when you look at it.
○ Light your candle and scatter a circle of salt – earth's natural elemental substance – around the base of the candle holder, seeing the strength of the majestic stone circles, huge standing stones, impenetrable castles and great temples that have survived the test of time.

Use your earth candle if you feel insecure, if you are wavering from a wise or necessary course, or if restlessness is preventing you from fulfilling opportunities.

Air

Air represents life itself, logic, the mind, communication, health, new beginnings, travel, learning and healing, and the male/yang/god in the form of sky deities.

If you have a large amount of air in your make-up, you are versatile and a good communicator, logical and always open to new ideas and opportunities.

Air's elemental creatures are sylphs, gentle spirits of the air who can be seen as butterflies and offer innovative ideas and a reminder to enjoy happiness while you can, rather than demanding guarantees or worrying about future problems that might never come to pass.

Colours Yellow, red **Quarter** East **Direction** Dawn **Season** Spring

Zodiacal signs Gemini, Libra, Aquarius

○ Surround your air candle with feathers, thistledown, tiny helium balloons, model planes and ceramic or wooden birds. Place the candle so that you face east to look at it.
○ Light your candle and waft incense, air's natural substance, nine times clockwise around the candle flame, feeling the mighty winds blowing, clouds skimming across the sky, birds soaring high, kites tugging at their strings; boats scudding across the water – promising expanding horizons both physical, mental and spiritual.

Use your air candle whenever you seek change or when lines of communication are blocked.

Fire

Fire represents light, the sun, lightning, fertility, power, joy, ambition, inspiration and achievement, and also destruction of what is no longer needed. Like air, fire represents the male/yang/god in the form of the sun deities.

If you have a large amount of fire in your make-up, you are dynamic, independent, inspirational, optimistic and creative.

The elemental creature of fire is the salamander, the mythical lizard, who lives within fire (though the name is now given to a species of amphibious newt). The salamander offers an understanding of mystical processes and visions to inspire future paths and ventures.

Colours Gold, orange **Quarter** South **Direction** Noonday sun **Season** Summer

Zodiacal signs Aries, Leo, Sagittarius

- Surround your fire candle with golden sunflowers or chrysanthemums, tiny mirrors that reflect the light and clear crystal quartz that is called in the Orient the 'essence of the dragon'. Place the candle so that you face south when you look at it.
- Light your candle and hold a gold-coloured taper in the candle flame for a moment, so that the two fires burn as one, seeing the brilliant sun at its full power, festival fires blazing on hilltops, volcanoes and golden fields of ripe corn, assuring you that if you strive, you will succeed.

Use your fire candle for inspiration, for joy and for energy.

Water

Water represents love, relationships, sympathy, intuition, healing, and the cycle of birth, death and rebirth. Like earth, water symbolizes the female/yin/goddess in the form of the moon goddesses.

If you have a large proportion of water in your make-up, you will be sensitive, intuitive, sympathetic and adaptable.

This element's creatures are undines, spirits of the water. The original Undine was created without a soul, but gained one by marrying a mortal and bearing him a child. However, she also lost her freedom from pain and her immortality, and so is a reminder that love may have a price, but that without it life does not have meaning.

Colours Blue, silver **Quarter** West **Direction** The setting sun **Season** Autumn

Zodiacal signs Cancer, Scorpio, Pisces

- Surround your water candle with silver objects, sea shells and pieces of coral or mother of pearl, bounty of the sea, and moonstones for the lunar goddesses, which grow brighter as the moon waxes. Anoint the candle with rose- or jasmine-scented oil for the water element. Place the candle so that you face west when you look at it.
- Light your candle, and as you do so see the sea crashing on rocks, and mighty waterfalls, but also gentle bubbling streams and still, deep lakes.

Use your water candle for kindling or rekindling love and for restoring harmony.

Elemental *candle protection*

In formal rituals, you can use the four elemental candles to call upon the protection of four archangels who traditionally represent the four directions and elements.

Whether or not you are creating a magical circle, use clockface positions to place the four elemental candles around you, so that the earth candle would be at a 12 o'clock position in the north, either using a compass to find magnetic north or by using a symbolic direction.

I have deliberately not described the archangels in detail, as each of us sees them in our own way.

Raphael

Raphael is the healer and travellers' guide, and so is often associated with Mercury. He is the angel who offers healing to the planet and to mankind, and to all creatures on the face of the earth, in the skies and in the waters. He is also guardian of the young. He is depicted with a pilgrim's stick, a wallet and a fish, showing the way and offering sustenance to all who ask.

Raphael stands in the north and is the angel of the night. He offers physical or emotional healing and reconciliation, and also an awareness that there must be endings if there are to be beginnings. Raphael can be felt most strongly on the midwinter solstice, around 21 December, and also at the beginning of the old northern winter on 1 November, still celebrated in Catholic countries as the day when departed family are remembered in a loving way and their lives celebrated.

Colour Green **Crystals** Jade, aquamarine **Incenses/oils** Myrrh, pine

○ Face the north, the direction of midnight.
○ Light a green candle, calling upon the healing wisdom and protection of Raphael with such words as:

> *Raphael, bringer of peace and nourishment, heal my sorrows and sustain me in my endeavours, so that I can walk in harmony with my fellow man. May the protective winds of the north guard me while I undertake my ritual and afterwards as I sleep.*

○ As you light the candle, visualize Raphael rising from the candle flame to stand sentinel as you carry out your rituals.

Uriel

Uriel, whose name means 'fire of god', is associated with earthquakes, storms and volcanoes and is the archangel of salvation. He warned Noah of the impending flood and led Abraham out of Ur. Believed to have given alchemy to mankind, he also imparted the wisdom of the Kabbalah to Hebrew mystics.

Uriel stands in the east and offers clarity and a fresh perspective, but may also herald necessary change. He is the angel of dawn and his special time is the spring equinox, around 21 March, which under the old Julian calendar was close to the New Year, until 1582 in Europe and 1752 in the UK.

OPPOSITE Candles representing earth, air, fire and water form an elemental circle of power and protection.

Colours Yellow, scarlet **Crystals** Carnelian, amber **Incenses/oils** Sandalwood, rosemary

○ Face the east, the direction of the rising sun.
○ Light a yellow candle, calling upon the transformative energies of Uriel with such words as:

> *Great Uriel, archangel of change and transformation, give me the courage to forge my destiny along the path of beauty and right action, without being deterred by obstacles or my own self-doubt. May the winds of the east offer me protection as I work and focus in my daily life to make necessary change.*

○ As you light the candle, visualize Uriel rising from the flame and standing in the east to protect you.

Michael

Sometimes called the archangel of the sun, Michael is the angel of light and the warrior angel. He appeared to Moses as the fire in the burning bush and saved Daniel from the lions' den. As commander of the heavenly hosts, Michael (who is pictured with a flaming sword) drove Satan and his fallen angels out of the celestial realms; as angel of judgement, he also carries a scale weighing the souls of the dead. According to the Koran, the cherubim were created from Michael's tears.

Michael's position is in the south with the noonday sun and he offers power to overcome any obstacles, wisdom, illumination and also challenge as to the right path.

Michael's feast day is 29 September, but you can feel his presence most vividly on May morning, famed for the St Michael sunrise – when in England, along a ley line (believed to be a line of psychic energy) stretching from Cornwall to East Anglia, the sun can be seen rising over the sun churches named after St Michael and St George (who was formerly linked with the northern sun god Og). Michael is also linked with the summer solstice or longest day, which is around 21 June.

Colours Gold, orange **Crystals** Citrine, pure crystal quartz **Incenses/oils** Frankincense, orange

○ Face the south, the direction of the noonday sun.
○ Light a gold candle, calling upon the light-bringing powers of Michael with such words as:

> *Mighty Michael, archangel of light and power, give me the inspiration to see my path clearly and the strength not to stray from it or weaken in my determination. May the warm winds of the south grant me protection as I undertake this ritual and the clarity thereafter to see the path ahead.*

○ As you light the candle, visualize Michael rising from the flame and standing in the south to guard you.

Gabriel

Sometimes called the archangel of the moon, the messenger archangel and the heavenly awakener, Gabriel appears many times in the Bible, visiting the Virgin Mary and her cousin Elizabeth, mother of John the Baptist, to tell them that they were to bear sons who would lead mankind to salvation. It was Gabriel who parted the waters of the Red Sea so that the Hebrews could escape from the Pharaoh's soldiers. Gabriel is usually pictured holding a sceptre or lily. To the followers of Islam, Gabriel is the spirit of truth who dictated the Koran to Mohammed.

Gabriel stands in the west, bringing wise words of truth and the clear voice that speaks of hope and a new purpose in life, but also compassion and the acceptance of the weaknesses of self as well as others. Gabriel can be felt with each new moon, especially on the day before the crescent is visible in the sky and on the autumn equinox, which falls around 21 September. The angel of evening, his or her feast day is 24 March.

Colour Silver **Crystals** Moonstone, fire opal **Incenses/oils** Jasmine, mimosa

○ Face finally the west, the direction of the setting sun.
○ Light a silver candle, calling upon the wise counsel of Gabriel, the messenger, saying such words as:

> *Wise Gabriel, let me hear your message as to the purpose of my life and the truths I must learn to achieve your mission for me and the compassion I must gain if I am to receive it. Protect me as I work and afterwards help me to follow my heart and not my sentiments. May the moist winds of the west protect me as I work and afterwards help me to follow my heart and not my sentiments.*

○ As you light the flame, visualize Gabriel rising from the flame in order to protect you.

Using your angelic protection

You can add to any archangel candle ritual by using the crystal and incense associated with each entity. In this way, you can create personal candle elemental rituals, focused on a specific archangel whose energies you need.

For general rituals you do not need to invoke each of the four archangels (unless you wish to do so), but can create a psychic shortcut whereby as you light each of the elemental candles and make a symbolic gesture, perhaps touching your heart, you automatically draw their love to you while you carry out your ceremony.

For this reason, I often light the four elemental candles, with or without casting a circle (see Chapter 16), as a way of creating a special and spiritual space for candle work.

Creating a Special Place for Candle Magic

Because candles are such a common decoration, you can discreetly set aside an area where you can keep candles and special objects to use for your candle rituals, meditation and divination. Whether you are interested in formal magical practices or want to use your candle ceremonies as they have been used for centuries as an extension of your everyday life, it is practical to keep all your candle materials in a single place. Even a small table or work surface prepared with candles, crystals and seasonal flowers or plants can be restorative in a busy life – an oasis of calm and order.

Some people have a special room or conservatory where they can withdraw to sit by candlelight, but if all you have is a coffee table in a shared living area or a chest of drawers in your bedroom, it is in itself a statement that your candle rituals – whether complex or simple – mark out an area of your life that is separate from other roles you play and demands on your time. Even if you can spend only ten minutes in the evening before bed lighting and gazing into your candle, you will find that you sleep better and feel less stressed and anxious in your daily world.

You may wish to invite friends or family members to share special celebrations such as the candle magic ritual on the new moon, described in Chapter 10. Children love candles and under supervision can also benefit not only from the use of candles on family celebrations, but by sharing simple ceremonies if they are sad or anxious.

A magical **place**

Begin with your altar or table. This can be circular, square or rectangular. A round altar, the shape of the sacred circle, works especially well.

You can adapt a table or chest of drawers, or construct a special altar that is used only for your candle rituals. A piece of unpolished wood such as hazel, ash, rowan or oak – all magical trees – or uncut stone supported on bricks will do.

During formal rituals where you have lit the four elemental candles or cast a circle, you will need to move all the way round, although some practitioners position the altar in the north of the circle and stand in the south facing it for all their work. You can keep the altar pushed against the wall for the rest of the time.

If you have a sheltered, private place in your garden or back yard, you can adapt a tree stump or flat rock as your work space. Picnic tables or benches are good basic structures. Use the benches for placing candles at different levels.

Preparing your special place

Even if you are using a communal room in a apartment or house, it is quite possible to leave your altar partly prepared, although items such as salt and water are best added just before a ritual. If you are subtle about placing the items, it will offer a focal point for the room. A garden altar can be set with an outdoor candle or torch and stone figurines, perhaps shaded by bushes.

CANDLES AND CANDLE HOLDERS

You will need two altar candles in white, cream or natural beeswax, from which you will light all the other candles used in rituals. These will be positioned so that items can be placed in the four compass points around them, and will be the first candles lit in any ritual, immediately after casting a circle, if you are using one. They are sometimes called the god candle (the left candle) and the goddess candle (the right candle); the latter is lit first.

There is debate over whether you should snuff or pinch out candles that you do not wish to burn. Candle snuffers are readily available, but the act of blowing out a candle is itself a magical release of power and rather than holding the light in a snuffer, you can send it forth to all who need it. This is an excellent way of releasing power at the end of a rite.

Candle holders can be wood, ceramic, glass, brass (the colour and metal of the sun) or silver (the colour and metal of the moon). They should be sufficiently solid to carry, and if they have a wide rim there will be no problem with dripping wax.

You ideally need at least six: two for the altar candles and four for the elements, plus two or three others to hold candles that represent people or wishes. These need not be elaborate – in fact, some of the finest magical rituals I have seen were done with candles in painted milk bottles.

Keep a supply of altar candles. These are sold as 'church candles' and range in width and length from 25cm (10in) to 1m (3ft). A septalite church candle burns for seven days and is good for rituals that last several days. You can divide the septalite into days by scratching six equally placed horizontal division marks with a nail or awl. Some candles have several wicks.

By the rules of strict ceremonial magic, you should never use a candle that has been lit for another ritual or purpose, and should not use these afterwards for household purposes. However, since candles are so expensive, and as you will only be performing positive magic, there is no reason why ritual candles should not be adapted for everyday use. After all, our forebears were not so fussy and asked for love, health and a good harvest using the candles that illuminated their homes. Use candles from harmony spells in quiet areas of the home, and those used for energy and success in work or study areas. Candles used for banishing magic are the only ones which should not be reused around the home. If you do wish to remove magical energies from a candle, circle a crystal pendulum over it nine times anti-clockwise and wash the pendulum under running water.

You will also need a supply of coloured candles, with one for each of the four ancient elements (see Chapter 15), to place on the actual or visualized line of the circle or at the compass points. (In some systems I have used, red is the colour of fire, but as long as you are consistent in your associations, the actual colours do not matter – both this and the colours given in Chapter 4 have worked at different times for me.) Light elemental candles after the altar candles, but before any wish or astrological candle, and begin in the north.

Keep candles in the colours of the rainbow, plus all the astrological colours, gold for solar magic, silver for lunar rituals, and white that will substitute for almost everything. Add basic scented candles – perhaps lavender, rose and sandalwood – that can cover most needs.

All this is not as much of a chore as it sounds. You can ask for candles as presents or buy them yourself as a souvenir.

CANDLE BOXES

From experience, I have learned that candles left lying loose invariably get cracked or chipped. Most churches still have an open wooden candle box on the wall that not only keeps candles safe, but shows if any colour is running low.

You can make or buy a free-standing or wall-mounted, long rectangular box in either wood or metal, or you can improvise by covering a large shoebox.

POWER STATUES

You may like to place statues between your altar candles – perhaps of a god and goddess figure from either your own spiritual background or from a culture that seems significant to you, to balance the male or yang energies and the female or